# Socialization as Education in a Cross-Cultural Revitalization Movement in Southern California

G. David Rath

UNIVERSITY PRESS OF AMERICA,® INC.
Lanham • Boulder • New York • Toronto • Plymouth, UK

**Copyright © 2009 by University Press of America,® Inc.**
4501 Forbes Boulevard
Suite 200
Lanham, Maryland 20706
UPA Acquisitions Department (301) 459-3366

Estover Road
Plymouth PL6 7PY United Kingdom

*All rights reserved.* Printed in the United States of America
British Library Cataloging in Publication Information Available

Library of Congress Control Number: 2009929102
ISBN: 978-0-7618-4653-6 (paperback : alk. paper)
eISBN: 978-0-7618-4654-3

Printed in the United States of America

∞™ The paper used in this publication meets the minimum requirements of American
National Standard for Information  Sciences—Permanence of Paper for Printed Library
Materials, ANSI Z39.48-1992

For the King of kings and Lord of lords (Colossians 1:17)

# Contents


Acknowledgments                                                                xi

1  Introduction                                                                 1
   Problem Statement                                                            2
   Research Questions                                                           2
      Limitations                                                              2
   Qigong and the History of Falun Gong                                        3
      The Qigong Boom                                                           4
      The Rise of Falun Gong                                                    5
      Roots of Estrangement                                                     5
   Falun Gong Goes Abroad                                                       6
      Crackdown                                                                 6
   Significance of the Study                                                    7
   Definitions                                                                 8
   Summary                                                                     12

2  Literature Review                                                          13
   Description without Theory                                                  13
   Nativistic Movements                                                       14
   Revitalization Theory                                                      15
   New Religious Movements                                                    18
   Relative Deprivation Theory                                                20
   Alienation, Deprivation, Modernization and Secularization                  21
   Rational Choice                                                            22
   Global Movements                                                           22
   Advantages of Globalization                                               23
   Religion                                                                   25

Brain Studies 25
Conclusion to Literature Review on Movements 28
Summary of Theoretical Literature in Regard to Falun Gong 28
Summary of Chapter 2 29

3 Research Design and Methodology 31
Qualitative Research 31
Grounded Theory Methodology 31
Data Collection 33
Validation Strategies 33
Role of the Researcher 34
Ethical considerations 35
Falun Gong Texts 36
Semi-Structured Interviews 36
Observations 37
Setting and Sample 37
Participants 37
Data Analysis 38
Delimitations 38
Limitations 39
Summary of Chapter 3 39

4 Results: Socialization per the Interviews 41
Conversion and Growth 42
Truth, Compassion and Tolerance 42
Five Exercises 44
Volunteerism 45
Sharing 45
Conversion Stories 45
Individual and Group Sharing 46
Demonstrations, Parades and Shows 47
Print and Sharing 48
Books and Sharing 48
Books and Growth 48
Newspapers 49
Telephones 50
E-mail 51
The Internet 51
Secular Media 52
FLG Media 52
Interconnected Technologies 53
Ming Hui School 53

Parents 53
The Principal 54
The Ming Hui Complementary Curriculum 56
Analysis of Ming Hui Content 59
Restoration 60
Summary of Chapter 4 60

5  Results: Socialization in FLG Media 63
Truth, Compassion and Tolerance 63
Compassion 65
Tolerance 66
The Internet 66
Five Exercises 67
Learning the Exercises from the Books 67
Learning the Exercises from the Internet 68
Learning the Exercises at the Parks 68
Nine Day Seminars 69
Volunteerism 69
Individual and Group Sharing 71
Demonstrations, Parades and Shows 71
Parades 72
Shows 72
Banknotes 74
Print and Sharing 74
Telephones 76
Cold Calling China 76
Funding the Cold Calling 78
Texting and Online Chatting 78
E-Mail 79
Marketing 79
Digital Guerilla Activity 80
Circumventing Firewalls 80
Digital Invasion 81
Declarations 81
Political Pressure and Networking with Other Groups 84
Lawsuits 84
Reports before Governments 85
Summary of Chapter 5 86

6  Ming Hui School 87
The Ming Hui Network 87
The Ming Hui Complementary Curriculum 88

The Ming Hui School Site						88
Sample Lesson Plan						89
Ming Hui Content						91
    Myth and Legend						91
    History							91
    Poetry and Drawing						91
    Science							94
Ming Hui Methodology						94
    Modern Methods						94
    Stories and Drama						95
    Teaching Methodology					95
    Multiple Intelligences					95
    Metacognition and Self-Assessment				96
    Traditional Method: Memorization				96
    Spirituality						96
Summary of Chapter 6						97

7. Comparing Ming Hui with Similar Schools			99
    Los Angeles Area Chinese School				99
    A Saturday Korean School					101
    The Kabbalah School: Spirituality for Kids			102
    Comparison and Contrast					105
    Summary of Chapter 7					106

8. Conclusion							109
    A Compelling New Vision for All				111
    Model of FLG Socialization					113
    Suggestions for Further Study				116
    Education and CCRMs					117
    What Educators Can Learn					118
    Principles of Educational Evaluation				120
    Educational Imperative					120
    Summary of Chapter 8					121

Appendix A Informed Consent Form (English)			123

Appendix B Informed Consent Form (Chinese)			125

Appendix C Questionnaire					127

Appendix D Phase One Interview Guide for Practitioners		128

Appendix E Phase Two Interview Guide for Practitioners		129

Appendix F Interview Guide for the Principal			130

Appendix G Interview Guide for Parents 131

References 133

Index 145

# Acknowledgments

Many persons have contributed to the success of this dissertation.

I am grateful to the participants in this study for spending hours describing, explaining and sharing their experiences, providing me with data and critique of the emerging grounded theory. This work is their story.

I am also deeply grateful to my family, without whose sacrifices, this research would not have begun, much less reached a conclusion. My parents, Charles and Lorraine Rath provided me with a "firm foundation" and constant affirmation. My sister, Linda L. Rath—also a grounded researcher—has always been available for suggestions, critique and support. My darling wife, Sarah, aided me in transcription and translation of Chinese interviews and Internet data. My friend Yi also provided speedy and helpful Chinese language consultation. My sons, Aaron and Josiah, willingly sacrificed much father-and-son-time so that I could conduct this research.

To my mentors at Biola University, I owe a deep debt of gratitude. Dr. Don Douglas spent untold hours with me—just me—storytelling and brainstorming until I finally arrived at my present topic.

My dissertation committee was extremely helpful throughout the entire process. Dr. Kevin Pittle provided me with many helpful suggestions and resources. Dr. Richard Starcher provided regular consultation on grounded theory methodology. And my committee chair, Dr. Douglas Hayward, not only affirmed my critique of existing theory but encouraged me to tinker and helped me to keep the purpose of this study clearly in focus every step of the way.

# Chapter One

# Introduction

With the arrival of spring came the requisite spring fever, which struck deep in the heart of every student sentenced to the concrete classroom in northern China. Sensitive to the students needs, indeed, infected myself, I asked my students if they would like to practice their English in the nearby city park. Delighted, the class surged out the door, out of the school gate and down the street, chattering in Chinese as they went.

Unlike the gray school and the gray city, the park was a maze of green swards and blazing flowers, which only added fuel to the pandemonium. I wondered if I would rue the decision to loose the students, who had completely forgotten the purpose of the excursion. They skipped and laughed in the sun until they came across a man dressed in white, who seemed, in slow motion, to be fighting an invisible enemy. Rapt, they watched the man until he completed his exercise. Then they were upon him. How long had he been practicing *qigong*? What kind of *qigong* was it? Could he impart some of his *qi* to them?

I never forgot this chance encounter, the delight of the students, and the stories they repeated of the miracles manifested by *qigong* practitioners. Years later, in a doctoral class investigating the educational philosophies of great religious traditions, I, now a student, was assigned a term paper, one that would examine how the philosophy of one of the great religious traditions informed its pedagogy. But realizing that the educational contributions of Christianity, Islam, Buddhism and Confucianism had been examined *ad nauseam*, I cast about for something less common and less well understood.

Taoism came to mind—that ancient religion and philosophy that had influenced Chinese culture in numerous ways. Yet Taoism was the subject of few educational works. Indeed, Taoism had not produced a formal educational structure, for Taoism was highly private, passed from one master to (usually) one student. Thus it was evident that Taoism would be extremely difficult to scrutinize. Yet further investigation revealed that Taoism had new offspring, a hitherto unknown form of *qigong—Falun Gong* (FLG). Not the private Taoism of old, FLG was practiced publicly in groups. Since its debut a few years ago, FLG has spread like Greek fire from China to cities around the world—despite the Chinese government's attempts to stamp it out.

## PROBLEM STATEMENT

Scholars have described FLG as a political movement (J. Li, 2006), a social movement (Penny, 2003), a revitalization movement (Ownby, 2000), a new religious movement (Lucas, 2004), and a spiritual movement (Tong, 2002). All these labels do apply, in part, yet they lack comprehensiveness. It seems that the present theoretical constructs are inadequate. What is still needed is a unifying theory addressing all of these issues and incorporating the socialization process, which all of these other theories ignore.

## RESEARCH QUESTIONS

This study will utilize grounded theory methodology (Glaser & Strauss, 2006) to answer the following question: How does the FLG educate/socialize its members into the FLG community? And what does this tell us about the nature of FLG as a social movement? Supporting research questions for this study are:

1. Why are people attracted to FLG?
2. How does FLG satisfy needs/reasons for conversion?
3. How does the FLG form a new cultural community?
4. How does the FLG recruit/instruct followers?
    A.  How are different educational methods used and why?
    B.  What are the various forms these methods take?
    C.  What is communicated through these methods?
    D.  How are these methods perceived?
5. How does education promote a new steady state?

### Limitations

1. Because this study utilized grounded theory methodology , a form of qualitative research, the data may be subject to interpretations other than my own.

2. The study produced a substantive level theory generalizable to the participants in the study, but it did not necessarily provide broad generalizability.


## QIGONG AND THE HISTORY OF FALUN GONG

FLG arose out of the *qigong* movement developed by the Chinese government in the 1950s. Indeed, the Chinese government created the term *qigong* (Ownby, 2000). The roots of this practice extend at least to White Lotus cults (Ownby, 2000), which were earlier amalgamations of the three major official religions in China (Confucianism, Buddhism and Taoism). Related cultivation systems, however, extend at least to the Warring States period in 5th century B.C. (Hsu, 2001; Slingerland, 2003). While there is little in the literature to explain the reason for the term White Lotus, according to Ownby, it has clearly been a derogatory term and a catchall phrase. Specific information on the various White Lotus cults remains scarce and vague because whenever possible, the Chinese government destroyed any such information, trying to stamp it out. Ownby believes a study of the FLG will likely shed light on the nature of these elusive White Lotus cults. That is not to say that the FLG and the White Lotus are synonymous, or even that the FLG is a descendent of the White Lotus. Rather, the cultural roots upon which these groups and the governments draw, and the great number of similarities and patterns of action, may aid in understanding of both the past and the present.

In the 1950s, the government of the People's Republic of China (PRC) created *qigong* in hopes of preserving the best of Chinese medicine, which seemed to be threatened by the westernization of Chinese medical practice, while culling the superstitious (read "religious") and feudal elements, which had been part and parcel of Chinese medicine since ancient times. The word *qigong* was formed from two Chinese words, *qì* (氣) meaning air or gas and *gōng* (功) meaning work or cultivation—the implication being that *qigong* was an exercise for working the air, or cultivating one's inner spirit or "cosmic breath." (Ownby, 2003b, p. 233) Hence, *qigong* was a set of mental and physical exercises designed to transform the constitution of one's body and to develop one's moral character. Depending on the form of *qigong*—as there are more than 400 varieties (Cui, 1989a)—these exercises may include breathing techniques, stylized gestures, and meditation (Wessinger, 2003).

During the Cultural Revolution, however, *qigong* institutions were destroyed, as *qigong* came to be viewed, *in toto*, as feudal. After the death of Mao Zedong, the hysteria of the Cultural Revolution subsided. So enthusiasts could practice *qigong*. Yet without institutional structure, they were left to their own devices—hence the rise of various *qigong* schools taught by charismatic *qigong* masters whose main goal was not stripping out feudalistic superstition.

The primary reason for the reemergence of *qigong*, though, was the "scientific discovery" of *qi* (Cui, 1989a; D. Palmer, 2005). This discovery lead, in 1983, to the establishment of the Chinese *Qigong* Scientific Research Association (CQSRA) (Cui, 1989b) to reduce health care costs, to restore ancient Chinese knowledge, and to distinguish scientific fact from superstition in *qigong* (Ownby, 2003a). *Qigong* was supposed to be a regimen of ancient exercises, including prescribed movements, postures, meditation and controlled breathing for healing, preventing illness, and increasing longevity. Before the 1950s, though, there was no practice known as *qigong*. And though there was a long history of spiritual exercises in relation to longevity, there certainly had been no scientific method to these practices. Yet many of the beliefs and practices in *qigong* are traceable to Chinese folk religion and traditional Chinese medicine (Ownby, 2007).


## The Qigong Boom

A number of magazines were "devoted to qigong research and popularization" (Cui, 1989a, p. 20). Besides being a subject of research, *qigong* became common in hospitals; classes were set up across China for the public; and universities offered *qigong* classes. The Chinese media, controlled by the government, touted *qigong* as a Chinese scientific panacea, enhancing concentration, memory, athletic ability and curing ulcers, high blood pressure, paralysis, and cancer (Cui, 1989a).

In 1989, the Chinese Qigong Scientific Research Association estimated that one in 20 Chinese, young and old, were practicing *qigong*. By 1990, the Chinese government estimated that there were 60 million practitioners of *qigong* (Ownby, 2003b). In fact, some scholars estimate that 200 million Chinese took part in the *qigong* boom (Ownby, 2007). The large population of China (over 1 billion in 1985) and the governmental and media backing make these numbers believable. *Qigong* was touted as being able to make the practitioner feel better, become healthy. The Chinese *Qigong* Scientific Research Association produced a great number of studies documenting the effects of practicing *qigong* and made these studies public, which made the practice even more popular. Meanwhile, throughout the country, different schools of *qigong* emerged as different masters became popular.

## The Rise of Falun Gong

Li Hong Zhi began teaching Falun Gong (法輪功) (FLG), aka Falun Dafa (法輪大法), in 1991. Here, the word *gōng* is the same as in *qigong*, implying that FLG is basically a form of *qigong*. However, the words *fǎ* (法) and *lún* (輪), making up the term *Falun*, literally mean "law" and "wheel," respectively, implying that there is a law and a wheel involved in the practice of FLG. The phrase *Dafa* in the name *Falun Dafa*, is literally "great law." As there is no previous record of this particular form of cultivation—*qigong* or otherwise—and as this particular movement has since become controversial, there are different accounts of where Li received his training. According to government sources, Li took *qigong* classes starting in 1988, but according to Li's autobiography, he studied under Buddhist and Taoist masters from the age of eight (Lu, 2005; Tong, 2002). In any case, Li began to teach FLG publicly as a form of *qigong* in May 1992, and in August 1993, the Falun Gong Research Society was officially registered under the Chinese *Qigong* Scientific Research Association.

In 1993, Li Hongzhi and several followers participated in the second Oriental Health Expo in Beijing, healed the sick, and Li became an instant star of the *qigong* movement (Lu, 2005; Ownby, 2003b). FLG was given the highest award at the Expo. And over the next year, FLG received honors from the police ministry and the CQSRA.

Between 1992 and 1994, Li gave 54 lectures to large audiences throughout China totaling at least 60,000 (Ownby, 2007). The government controlled radio and television media even provided Li a platform with in-depth interviews and FLG radio shows across the country (Awards, 2008). FLG, led by Li Hong Zhi, soon became the most popular form of *qigong* in the PRC. He began to offer free lectures and forbade FLG practitioners from charging any fees. This move added to his popularity among enthusiasts, but upset the masters of other *qigong* schools and the CQSRA who asked him to increase his tuition, which he refused (Schechter, 2001). In fact, in 1994 Li no longer conducted training sessions in China—which were marketed through the CQSRA—to "devote his time to the study of Buddhism" (Tong, 2002).


## Roots of Estrangement

That same year, Li's *Zhuan Falun* (H. Li, 2003) was published in which he stated that he would no longer use *qigong* to heal others because healing was a low level goal. Rather, he would enable those who truly came to "learn the law" (p. 2), the Buddha Law, to eliminate their own Karma, the underlying cause of health problems and suffering. His recurring theme of the dangers of demons and possessing spirits is clearly a departure from what the communist state would accept as science.

Then in March 1996, Li instructed his lieutenants to officially withdraw FLG from the CQSRA (Chronicle, 2004; Human Rights Watch Report, 2002). This same year, the tide began to turn as the Chinese government began to crack down on *qigong* as false science, prohibiting its use for healing and exacting eight million Yuan in fines from a *qigong* organization in Suzhou (Tong, 2002). Li had heard rumors that influential people had compared the rise of FLG to the notorious Boxer rebellion (Ownby, 2007). So in October 1997, Li left China on a tourist visa for the United States and began applying for an immigrant visa, which he received in February 1998.


## FALUN GONG GOES ABROAD

It is unclear to what extent the above events were influenced by Li's activities abroad, but it is noteworthy that Li was teaching FLG abroad as early as March 1995. He was invited by the Chinese ambassador to France to share his teaching with the French. While there, Li lectured at the embassy and taught an evening class for several days at the cultural center of the Chinese embassy. He also lectured in Gothenburg (Göteborg), Sweden and Hong Kong (then a British colony) during the following two months. The next year, Li lectured in Sydney, Australia; Bangkok, Thailand; Houston, Texas; and New York City; and in addition, he presided over an international Falun Dafa conference in Beijing (Chronicle, 2004). This conference took place at about the same time that former Falun Gong Research Association members filed a report to the Chinese Ministry of Civil Administration and the Chinese Public Security Ministry indicating that they would not continue to apply for a formal Falun Dafa Association.


### Crackdown

In mid April 1999, after a Tianjin journal defamed *qigong* and FLG, practitioners protested. Riot police were sent to beat the demonstrators, arresting 45 (Ownby, 2007). Days later, on April 25, thousands of practitioners from around the country appeared early in the morning outside Zhongnanhai, the central headquarters for the Communist Party of China in Beijing, waiting quietly for a chance to ask to be left alone to practice their exercises without harassment. After a few hours, Premier Zhu Rongji took time to listen to their representatives and the crowd slowly dispersed, believing they had been heard.

Reportedly, the same evening, Jiang Zemin wrote a letter to the Political Bureau of the Central Committee of the Chinese Communist Party saying, "If the Chinese Communist Party cannot defeat Falun Gong, it will be the biggest joke on earth" (Chronicle, 2004, ¶ 153). Two days later, in Dalian City, 10,000 practitioners gathered at the practice site to show support for the FLG's appeal to the government. Over the next few days, there was a FLG conference in Sydney (May 1-2) and Li Hongzhi was interviewed by the Chinese and English media. Then he traveled to Toronto where, on May 23, he lectured. On May 30, Falun Gong practitioners launched two FLG websites: Clearwisdom.net and Minghui.org.

On June 6, 1999, hundreds of FLG practitioners were interrogated, and on June 7, Jiang Zemin made a speech identifying FLG as a political threat, equal to the 1989 student movement at Tiananmen Square (Chronicle, 2004). Since then, FLG has been labeled an "evil cult" (Ownby, 2003b). In order to eradicate it, the 610 office has been especially established, having over 10,000 local offices and authority overriding ordinary government agencies. In order to avoid prison and torture, practitioners must sign a document promising not to practice FLG.

Many of those put in prison for practicing FLG and those who remained free have continued to surreptitiously practice and teach others. Today, FLG is practiced not only in China, where it continues to be banned, but in numerous sites around the world, including Southern California—the location of this study.

Many observers have noted that the spreading of FLG around the world and the use of the Internet and other advanced technologies has helped counterbalance the onslaught of the Chinese government. Of course, this situation only raises more questions. What is the role of these technologies in the growth and development of FLG? What fuels FLG's numerical growth outside of China, which has been primarily among Chinese who began practicing FLG abroad (Ownby, 2003a)? How is doctrine instilled? How does FLG maintain and develop itself in the face of competing paradigms (science, capitalism, socialism, and other religions)? This study will attempt to answer these more specific questions as well as the more general ones listed earlier.


## SIGNIFICANCE OF THE STUDY

The reason for focusing this study on the FLG's educational methodology is that there is little research on the FLG, the theories used to explain the movement are only a partial fit, and none of the research addresses educational questions. Furthermore, not only will such a study add to the knowledge about this particular movement, but also to the theories for explaining and predicting political movements, social movements, revitalization movements, new religious movements (NRMs) and spiritual movements. Though researchers employing various movement theories have provided rich description of movements, of their histories, and of narratives told within the movements, none have suggested a theoretical framework addressing education, nor indeed given much attention to how adherents are socialized into and within movements. There is a fair amount of work on socialization among cults that brainwash prospective adherents, but many movements do not brainwash adherents. FLG clearly does not. In short, education and socialization are largely unexplored. Hence, the addition of an educational perspective stands to address a remaining problem.

## DEFINITIONS

Because this study is cross-disciplinary, there are a number of terms that may be confusing to educators, to specialists in the study of religion, and to anthropologists. Furthermore, Falun Gong redefines a number of words used in common, as well as specialized, parlance. Unless otherwise indicated, the following definitions will be used:

1. *Buddha Law* (佛法, *fó fǎ;* or *Buddha Fa*; see also, *Falun Dafa* and *Falun Gong*), as used in the various FLG media, is the cosmic law of the universe based on the principles of truthfulness, compassion and tolerance. (H. Li, 2003) Practicing Falun Gong is the way to act in accordance with Buddha Law. Buddha Law must not to be confused with the law of Buddhism which Master Li claims was corrupted by the disciples of Sakyamuni after he died.

2. *Character* (also *mind-nature*; see *temperament)*

3. *Compassion* is, for English speakers, the desire to relieve the suffering of another, ultimately from the Latin, *com* meaning "together" and *pati* "to suffer," literally "to suffer with." The Chinese word for compassion tends to be more about action than feeling; *shàn* (善), means *good, virtuous, friendly, kind.* In FLG, *shàn* (善) is most often translated as *compassion,* though *benevolence* and *good* are also common. In the *Zhuan Falun,* Master Li explains the nature of compassion as the desire to save others:

Cultivation of Good can develop a heart of great compassion, and once this heart of great compassion comes out you can see that all sentient beings are suffering, so you'll be filled with one wish: to save all sentient beings. (H. Li, 2003, p. 8)

4. *Conversion* means to become. Feedback from participants showed initial dissatisfaction with the term conversion because, to them, conversion implies rejecting one's former religion and adopting another religion. They pointed out that many practitioners were atheists before becoming practitioners. Furthermore, practitioners note that Master Li says Falun Gong is not a religion. The practitioners were, however, satisfied with the term *conversion* meaning "to become, as in becoming a practitioner."

5. *Cult*, in common parlance, tends to take on a negative connotation. For example, the first definition for *cult* in *The American Heritage Dictionary* is as follows: "A religion or religious sect generally considered to be extremist or false, with its followers often living in an unconventional manner under the guidance of an authoritarian, charismatic leader." (Cult, 2000). What is meant by *cult* in this study, however, is anthropological in nature. For example, anthropologist Anthony Wallace defines a cult institution "as a set of rituals all having the same general goal, all explicitly rationalized by a set of similar or related beliefs, and all supported by the same social group." (1966, p. 75). In other words, a *cult* is a group of people who have the same set of beliefs and practices supporting the same goal (see also *Religion*).

6. *Dàfǎ* (大法), literally "great law," is an abbreviated form standing for the entire phrase "Falun Dafa" (H. Li, 2003).

7. *Divine Performing Arts* is the name of a dance troupe. The name in Chinese is *shényùn* (神韻 *shén* literally meaning *god, mysterious, soul or spirit* and *yùn* meaning *rhyme* or *likeness*). *Shényùn* is a term used in the arts to describe an esthetic value, expressing genuine feeling and sensitivity—natural and authentic, surpassing mere form and technique.

8. *Gōng* (功) is literally *work*. In the context of *qigong*, *gōng* is the cultivation of *qì* (氣), which is thus caused to spiral around the body and above the head in a column that transforms the body and mind to a higher level of existence. In *Zhuan Falun*, Master Li declares that *gōng* comes from cultivating one's character (H. Li, 2003).

9. *Fǎ* (法), law can refer to human laws established by governments. However, in Falun Gong, *Fǎ* refers to the law of the universe, the Buddha law—truthfulness, compassion and tolerance (H. Li, 2003).

10. *Falun, w*heel of the law, or law-wheel, from *fǎ* (法, law), and *lún* (輪, *wheel*). The falun is a law body symbolizing the universe in miniature, made available to the public by Master Li (H. Li, 2003). The falun rotates clockwise to absorb energy from the universe to evolve the practitioner's body and counterclockwise to send out used energy to benefit others nearby.

11. *Falun Dafa* (法輪大法) is literally "law-wheel great law," implying that Falun Gong far exceeds other forms of cultivation (H. Li, 2003). The

phrase *Falun Dafa*, though used interchangeably with Falun Gong, is preferred by Falun Gong practitioners. The repetition of the term *fǎ* (法, law) seems to imply more of a focus on cosmology than on exercises (see also, *Falun Gong* and *Buddha Law*).

12. *Falun Gong* (or *Falungong*; see also *Falun Dafa* and *Buddha Law*)

13. Falun Gong (法輪功), literally "Law Wheel Qigong," is a type of cultivation that increases the practitioner's energy even when not meditating because the Falun, which is placed in the practitioner's abdomen unceasingly transforms energy from the universe to save the practitioner and others. (H. Li, 2003)

14. *Karma* (Sanskrit for *deed* or *action*) in Hinduism and Buddhism refers to how one's thoughts and actions bring about one's condition through reincarnation and suffering (Krishan, 1997). It tends to be seen as an impersonal force that is too complex to understand. Bad karma keeps an individual in the cycle of reincarnation until retribution has been completed. In FLG, the principle of karma is similar to the above except that it is not an impersonal force. Rather it is defined as black matter, though in a different dimension. This black matter must be turned into white matter (virtue) through cultivation, which includes right thoughts and actions, the five exercises and suffering. Karma, however, is the reason for one's present level. In *Zhuan Falun*, Master Li explains how karma determines one's level:

    In this universe all things, and this includes even all the matter that permeates the whole universe, they're all living entities, they all have thinking, and they're all forms that the Law of the universe exists in at different levels. If they don't let you rise to a higher level, maybe you want to go higher, but you just can't go up, they just won't let you come up. And why don't they? Because your character hasn't improved. Every level has different standards, and if you want to raise your level, you have to put a stop to your bad thoughts and dump out your filth, and you have to assimilate to that level's standard. That's the only way you can go up. (H. Li, 2003, p. 14)

15. *Level*: Of the two phrases in FLG generally translated as *level* (水平, *shuǐ píng* and 階層, *jiē céng*), the latter is more telling. The former is more generic implying measurement of number, size or quality, as in production level. The latter (階層 *jiē céng*) implies of hierarchy or social stratum. Practicing FLG not merely improves one's body and character, but also position in the cosmos.

16. *Lún* (輪), *wheel*. *Lún* can refer to the wheel of a vehicle. However, in Falun Gong, it is the second word in the noun phrase *falun*, referring to the law body placed within a practitioner's body for transforming character.

17. *Mind-nature* (also c*haracter*; see *temperament)*

18. *Ming Hui:* the phrase *míng huì* (明慧) may be translated *wise* or *having clear insight*. The first ideogram in the phrase, 明, means clear, bright, having understanding. The second ideogram,慧, means intelligent. The phrase *míng huì* (明慧) is not a technical term in the practice of FLG, but it is the name of the weekend school for children run by FLG practitioners in Southern California and in many other cities around the world.

19. *Qì* (氣), air, gas, inner spirit or "cosmic breath" (Ownby, 2003b, p. 233).

20. *Qigong*, from *qì* (氣) and *gōng* (功) meaning work, is a set of mental and physical exercises designed to transform constitution of one's body and to develop one's moral character.

21. *Rectifying the Fa*: Rectifying the *Fa* is establishing the principle of truthfulness, compassion and tolerance in the human world and the cosmos. Only Master Li can rectify the Fa. Practitioners participate through a related process (see *validating the Fa*).

22. *Religion*, according to anthropologist Morton Klass, is the "process of interaction among the members of that society—and between them and the universe at large as they conceive it to be constituted—which provides them with meaning, coherence, direction, unity, easement, and whatever degree of control over events they perceive as possible" (Klass, 1995, p. 38). For a roughly synonymous term, see the entry on *cult*.

23. *Shényùn* (see *Divine Performing Arts*神韻)

24. *Temperament* (also *character* or *mind-nature*): the Chinese phrase心性 (*xīn xìng*), translated as *temperament*, is made of心 (*xīn*, meaning *heart, mind* or *soul*) and性 (*xìng*, meaning *nature* or *character*). The character of the person.

25. *Tolerance (*also *endurance, forbearance):* The character忍 (*rěn*) may be variously translated as *endure, persevere, bear, suffer,* or *forbear*. The radical component, 心 (*xīn*), means heart, mind, intelligence, soul. The phonetic component, 刃 (*rèn*), however, carrying more than just the associated sound, adds a sense of pain or suffering, as it also represents an edged tool, such as a knife, just over the heart. Hence, 忍 (*rěn*) may refer to anything that hurts deeply but is to be endured.
    In FLG media, 忍 (*rěn*) is translated *tolerance, forbearance* or *endurance*. In this study, these three words are treated as synonymous. In the interviews in this study, 忍 (*rěn*) is translated as tolerance because it fits more squarely with current American parlance. However, the most common meaning of tolerance in present American English has a more "live and let live" connotation. In FLG, though, tolerance has more to do with personal suffering. The immediate origin of the suffering may be sickness, persecution, one's own character flaw, or even sitting in

the lotus position during meditation (which can be painful). The root problem, though, is karma. The goal is to transform karma into "white matter" (virtue) through tolerating suffering. Master Li explains, "You get white matter when you've endured hardships, suffered, or done good things" (H. Li, 2003, p. 182). Tolerance, however, is no masochism; it is an equilibrium of the mind. Master Li says that if someone humiliates a practitioner, "maybe you can endure it but you can't get it off your mind. That's not good enough. You know, when a person reaches the Arhat level he's not fazed by anything he comes across" (p. 190).

26. *Truth*: In FLG, truth is a fundamental principle or law of the universe. Truth is not limited to what can be verified empirically or scientifically. Yet as practitioners gain experience with the paranormal, the veracity of FLG is authenticated.

27. *Validating the Fa*: Validating the *Fa* is establishing the principle of truthfulness, compassion and tolerance in the human world. When practitioners validate the Fa, Master Li is able to save them.

28. *Zhuan Falun*: Master Li's *Zhuan Falun* (2003) is the central text in FLG, focusing on cultivation in the larger sense, explaining how the exercises fit into the overall worldview.


## SUMMARY

In this introduction, I discussed the *qigong* movement in China, the rise of Falun Gong and the reasons for its popularity (the belief that this was an ancient Chinese science and that it benefited health). Further, popularity was enhanced by early government support and the media. I also discussed the Chinese government's crackdown on Falun Gong and its spread to numerous parts of the world. Further, I discussed how present theories have not adequately addressed how new religious movements socialize converts. Finally, operational definitions of Falun Gong were provided. The next chapter will entail a review of the academic literature on various types of social movements, the reasons for the rise of movements, and the strengths and weaknesses of existing theories.

*Chapter Two*

# Literature Review

This chapter will review the strengths and weaknesses of predominant theories from anthropology, sociology and the study of religion for explaining new religious movements—most importantly for explaining the FLG, the focus of this study. Historically, new movements have been described in five basic ways—as nativistic movements, revitalization movements, new religious movements (NRMs), socio-political movements, and, most recently, global movements. Not only in question is which theory is most fitting, or even how to combine the theories, but how adequate is any extant theory or combination of theories? This chapter will conclude by revisiting revitalization theory (Wallace, 1956), and by discussing how a grounded theory of Falun Gong education may make revitalization theory more complete.

## DESCRIPTION WITHOUT THEORY

One strategy in research is to ignore theoretical problems by focusing attention on description. One study, for example, (Chan, 2004) describes three types of FLG followers in Hong Kong and Chicago: core followers, ordinary followers and peripheral practitioners. According to Chan, core followers are those with the highest level of commitment in practicing FLG exercises and are convinced of the authority of Li Hong Zhi and the *Zhuan Falun*, the central text in FLG. Ordinary followers are those generally committed to FLG but also have some doubts. Those who are attracted to FLG because it is simple and free of charge, she labels peripheral practitioners.

Chan's (2004) analysis is descriptively helpful, but it does not explain the international growth, nor investigate differences between the different FLG groups. So though we might consider her research to be descriptively ground-breaking, the theory provided is quite limited in scope. Assuming that FLG is a new religious movement (NRM), she uncritically applies NRM theory and proceeds to describe how the movement fits existing theory. For example, she says FLG is cult-like because "most [members] are without any previous religious experiences" (p. 673). This statement is not borne out by the data of several studies (Ownby, 2003a; Porter, 2005), including this study. She also points out that FLG echoes Confucian teaching, reaching back to past mean-ings and values that have been lost by the present culture. This fact supports revitalization theory more closely than NRM theory. Finally, she concludes that the concepts developed in the West are inadequate for explaining FLG. Yet she offers no unified theory.

Chan does not address whether or not conversions outside of China are mo-tivated differently from those of practitioners in China. Nor does she address how doctrine is instilled, or how FLG maintains and develops itself in the face of competing paradigms (science, capitalism, socialism, and other religions). Without addressing these questions, there is no hope of explaining or predicting most of the phenomena in FLG. Further, extensibility to other movements is virtually non-existent. In short, for her, description is the focus, not theory.

## NATIVISTIC MOVEMENTS

Ralph Linton (1943) defines the first cogent typology of nativistic movements as "any conscious, organized attempt on the part of a society's members to revive or perpetuate selected aspects of its culture" (p. 230). He suggests that there are four possible types of nativistic movements: revivalistic-magical (as in the ghost dance), revivalistic-rational (as in the sun dance), perpetu-ative-magical (no examples provided), and the perpetuative-rational (which includes most dominant superior groups, as in Europeans' sending children back to Europe for schooling).

According to Linton, in order for nativistic movements to occur, there must be one of four scenarios: (a) a politically dominant society comes in contact with a culturally superior one (as in the nomads who conquered China); (b) a politically dominant society comes in contact with a culturally inferior one (as in the Romans v. Goths); (c) a politically dominated society comes in contact with a culturally superior one (none provided, but perhaps the Aztecs v. the Spanish); (d) a politically dominated society comes in contact with a culturally inferior one (industrialized cultures v. tribal cultures).

A significant problem with Linton's typology is his assumption that ratio-nal is superior to magical. Not only is such a characterization patronizing, but it fails to acknowledge its own epistemological supposition, i.e.,—that magic is both irrational and ineffectual (an unproven assumption). This assumption ignores a great many scientifically unexplainable phenomena that have been observed in regard to the practice of magic.

Perhaps Linton's reason for this error in typology is that he is not aware of any effective magical movement. In fact, Linton questioned whether any nativistic movement could be considered rational, "since all such movements are, to some extent, unrealistic" (Linton, 1943, p. 232). This last statement, though revealing about the positivism of Linton's day, does not, in itself, relegate the typology to the museum. It does, however, remind today's reader of how limiting positivism can be—that the real and the rational must be measurable, quantifiable and verifiable. Anything else would be considered unrealistic and irrational.

In fact, Linton provides no objective instrument for distinguishing between inferior and superior cultures. The terms lack definition. Anyone using this taxonomy could make a value judgment based on any number of personal preferences. Nevertheless, Linton's contribution lies in an attempt to delineate the factors that describe and predict the actions of cultures in conflict based on whether they are revivalistic, magical, perpetuative, or rational. Perhaps the term *rationalizing* would be more descriptive than the term *rational*—which embraces positivism's blind-spot. Finally, there may be other important factors that account for the rise and dynamics of nativistic movements. These factors will be explored in the following sections.

## REVITALIZATION THEORY

In his classic article, *Revitalization Movements*, anthropologist Anthony Wallace (1956) proposed a new theory to describe several types of societies, labeling them "revitalization movements" (p. 264). Wallace defined a revitalization movement as a "deliberate, organized, conscious effort by members of a society to create a more satisfying culture" (p. 265). For a society to function, each member "must maintain a mental image of the society and its culture" (p. 266). This mental image, which he calls a mazeway, enables individuals "to act in ways which reduce stress at all levels of the system . . . the mazeway is nature, society, culture, personality, and body image, as seen by one person" (p. 266). When the mazeway within a large portion of a society breaks down, revitalization movements are likely to occur.

Revitalization is a sequential process of five major periods through which a society goes: steady state, increased individual stress, cultural distortion, revitalization, steady state. The period of steady state is characterized by "culturally recognized techniques for satisfying needs operate with such efficiency that chronic stress within the system varies within tolerable limits (Wallace, 1956, p. 268). The period of individual stress occurs when individual members "experience increasingly severe stress as a result of the decreasing efficiency of certain stress-reduction techniques. . . . Admission that a major technique is worthless is extremely threatening because it implies that the whole mazeway system may be inadequate" (p. 269). With increasing stress, a period of cultural distortion occurs. Individuals respond to cultural distortion in three ways: toleration, instead of making "systematic adaptive changes in the mazeway"; making "limited mazeway changes in their personal lives"; or turning "to psychodynamically regressive innovations (p. 269). During the period of revitalization there are "six major tasks" (p. 270) which must be accomplished: (a) Mazeway reformulation: a prophet reformulates the mazeway; (b) Communication: the prophet communicates "his revelations to the people" (p. 273); (c) Organization: as individuals convert, "a small clique of special disciples…clusters about the prophet and an embryonic campaign organization develops with three orders of personnel: the prophet; the disciples; and the followers" (p. 273); (d) Adaptation: resistance is usually determined and resourceful. The movement may "have to use various strategies of adaptation: doctrinal modification; political and diplomatic maneuver; and force" (p. 274); (e) Cultural transformation: "a controlling portion of the population comes to accept the new religion" (p. 275); (f) Routinization: "If the group action program in nonritual spheres is effective in reducing stress-generating situations, it becomes established as normal in various economic, social, and political institutions and customs. . . . The organization contracts and maintains responsibility only for the preservation of doctrine and the performance of ritual" (p. 275). Finally, a new steady state is achieved as the cultural transformation completes by proving itself viable and by solving "its problems of routinization" (p. 275).

Wallace's examples of revitalization include not only nativistic, peyote and millenarist movements, but also cults (for the definition, see Chapter One), the Protestant Reformation, the American Revolution, and the Tai Ping Rebellion in China. Though Wallace's primary work has been with Native Americans (i.e., the Handsome Lake movement, the Ghost dance, and the Warmhouse movement), he suggested that everyone at some point in life participates in or encounters a revitalization movement. Though the theory is now fifty years old, anthropologists still use revitalization movements as a theoretical frame of reference to describe both historical and modern movements around the world, from Kenya (Kushner, 1965), to South Africa (Els, 1990), Malaysia (Kent, 2006), Singapore (Kuo, 1992), Guatemala (Warren, 1998), Eastern Europe (Ross, 2006), and to the islands of Melanesia (Stephen, 1997).

Nevertheless, there is some question—Wallace (2004) himself raises it—whether revitalization theory applies only to cultures reacting to the stresses involved with colonization (p. ix). Revitalization movement theory may necessarily be relegated to describing movements of the past because colonization is rapidly becoming a phenomenon of the past. Hence, there is some discussion as to whether the theory of revitalization can continue to describe other types of societies, especially those of today.

Colonization, however, is not required for revitalization. Though Wallace's work was primarily with Native Americans, his theoretical construct was developed with a wide array of cultures in mind, even the United States. With this question in mind, one study attempted to fit American history into revitalization theory. McLoughlin (1978), applying Wallace's revitalization theory to American history from 1607-1977, finds awakenings: the Puritan awakening (1610-1640), the First Great Awakening (the American Revolution, 1730-1760), Second Great Awakening (Jacksonian Democracy, 1800-1830), the Third Great Awakening of Progressivism (1880-1920), and the Fourth Great Awakening of pluralism, which he describes as the "failure of liberalism" (p. 179)—exemplified in nativism, social justice movements, rock concerts, drug use, the occult, and eastern mysticism. McLoughlin says that awakenings take a generation to come to fruition as the young must "escape the enculturation of the old ways" (p. 216).

While reform is mere structural within organizations, and revivals are merely alterations of the lives of individuals, awakenings (a particular form of revitalization) are "periods of cultural revitalization that begin in a general crisis of beliefs and values and extend over a period of a generation or so, during which time a profound reorientation in beliefs and values takes place" (McLoughlin, 1978, p. xiii). Of course, there are problems with fitting these awakenings into revitalization theory. First, the level of cultural distortion among white Americans can hardly compare with the distortion experienced by the Seneca, bringing about the Handsome Lake movement. Second, white America was never as ethnically or religiously homogenous as the Seneca. Third, as cultural crisis produces revitalization, why does McLoughlin not include the Civil War?

The first and second problems might be explained merely as a lower boiling point. Perhaps a lower level of distortion is required for larger, less homogeneous cultures. Further, it may be that where revitalization produces a small change in such a less homogeneous culture, the likelihood increases that another revitalization movement may soon follow. The third problem does not seem a conflict with the theoretical construct, but with McLoughlin's religious focus. Indeed, the Civil War might be described as nativistic in the South's desire to eliminate federalism from the mazeway, and the North's reinforcement of federalism could be described as millennial, especially when combined with the growing notion of manifest destiny.

In order to discuss the usefulness of revitalization theory, anthropologist M. E. Harkin (2004) invited twelve anthropologists to submit their research in relation to revitalization. Some anthropologists suggested areas where the theory needs refining. For example, Jukka Siikala criticizes the theory for beginning and ending with "a steady state of the society" (2004, p. 88) but never defining society or "the needs or the nature of culture" (p. 88). Further, Ann McMullen conjectures that another "undefined aspect of revitalization movements" (2004, p. 272) is whether they are events or processes. Another area wherein the theory of revitalization movements proves inadequate is in explaining differing outcomes of neighboring communities. Jason Baird Jackson (2004) wonders, "how . . . can the same religious tradition be a revitalization movement in one community and not one in another" (p. 188). Wallace is open to the possibility of "modifying the structure of revitalization theory itself" (2004, pp. viii), but he is far from abandoning it. In fact, he suggests that the present work on smaller revitalization movements "may still provide a model for the understanding of revitalization processes in larger polities that are profoundly affecting the contemporary world" (p. x).

It is precisely here—the need for applying revitalization theory to larger societies, perhaps even globally—that a study of the FLG may be of enormous benefit in understanding revitalization movements. Although FLG practitioners are relatively few in Southern California—compared to the many other spiritual practices in the area—they are part of a worldwide movement that has grown from zero in 1992 to at least 100 million around the world (Lowe, 2003). It is intriguing how FLG adherents maintain their connection with practitioners in China, where the practice of FLG is outlawed and severely punished. As of May 2008, a FLG website states that 3,158 practitioners have been killed, untold thousands imprisoned or sent to psychiatric hospitals and over 100,000 sent to forced labor camps (Gruesome, 2008).


## NEW RELIGIOUS MOVEMENTS


The study of new religious movements (NRMs) tends to focus on movements beginning in the West among Westerners borrowing religious practices from the East. The initial objection in using a theory from the field of NRMs to describe the FLG is that the FLG began in the East based on Eastern practices. This study does look at the FLG in Southern California, but it cannot ignore that this new movement is 100% Eastern in origin and appeals primarily to Chinese expatriates. Nevertheless, there is a sizable percentage of non-Chinese, approximately 10% (Ownby, 2003a), who participate in FLG. Hence, from the outset, there is a question of the suitability of analyzing the FLG from this perspective.

Furthermore, the term *religious* is suspect. Is FLG, for example, a religion? Many scholars (Dubuisson, 2003; Hinnells, 2005) would argue that the concept of religion is a western construct. Yet using the term *social movement* tends to relegate the discussion to the political arena, ignoring the spiritual elements and motivations within movements.

Early studies in NRMs in America tended to focus on three types of group: Eastern mysticism/guru movements, Christian hippie/Jesus movements, and religiotherapeutic/New Age groups (Robbins, 2000). Over the last 30 years, new theories, typologies and methodological advances have been rare (Beckford, 2000). However, the central theoretical constructs tend to be relative deprivation, secularization, rational choice and, increasingly, globalization—see the following sections. Yet there is still controversy as to what constitutes a new religion.

Perhaps Hexham and Poewe (1998) have offered the best solution by suggesting that much of what passes for a NRM is actually a revitalization movement within an established religion, not a new religion. They suggest that an authentic NRM produces a theology that is distinctly new and that borrows elements from different cultures, hence the term *global* in their title. However, in their view, a globalized network is not required for a movement to be designated as an NRM.

Another controversy is how to explain violence in some NRMs. Most writers suggest a dualism of "extrinsic or exogenous vs. intrinsic or endogenous sources of violence and volatility" (Robbins, 2000, p. 519). An extrinsic source of violence suggests persecution or provocation, while an intrinsic source of violence suggests latent tendencies in the movement—such as an apocalyptic worldview. The problem with this concept is that the same intrinsic and extrinsic motivations that produce violence in one group do not produce violence in another. For example, not all highly conservative Muslim groups resort to violence, nor do all Japanese NRMs. Yet these factors do figure in Wahhabism (Algar, 2002) and in the Aum Shinrikyo movement (Lifton, 2000).

Sociologists have tended to perceive new religions as small groups that are sociologically marginal, deviant, and "on the fringes of society" (Saliba, 1996, p. 7). However, the data on many new movements do not support this hypothesis. The FLG, for example, has been, and continues to be, made up of individuals from all echelons of society. (Schechter, 2001)

Despite all these drawbacks, these constructs are not without merit and should be considered as possible themes when analyzing a movement.

## RELATIVE DEPRIVATION THEORY

A common construct for explaining the rise of new movements is relative deprivation (RD) theory, with roots as far back as Marx and de Tocqueville. In general, RD suggests that new movements arise when individuals or groups feel that they are being deprived of something to which they are entitled. David Aberle (1960, 1982) posits three situations that constitute RD: a discrepancy between one's past and present circumstances; between one's present and future circumstances; and between one's own and someone else's circumstances. Classification of deprivations includes possessions, status, behavior, worth, and—added later—power (Aberle, 1982). This last seems to be something of a catchall, reinforcing his conviction that perceived loss of power, economic relations and resources trigger the rise of social movements.

Aberle's contribution to the discussion is helpful, especially in that not only does he provide description of movements within the Navajo, but taxonomic elements useful in describing other groups. Nevertheless, this taxonomy has flaws: an inability to predict (a) when and where a movement will arise, (b) what methods the movement will use (action or ritual) and (c) what the aims of such a movement will be (changing self or the world).

Charles Glock (1964) proposed five types of felt deprivation: economic (access to wealth), social (restrictions), organismic (stigmatizing physical handicap), ethical (rejecting dominant values), and psychic (search for meaning/new philosophy of life). Each of which produce a different type of religious group, respectively: sect, church, healing movement, reform movement, or cult. What is lacking in this theory is a consideration for social networking (Hak, 1998) and the importance an individual attaches to religion (Wimberley, 1989). Deprivation theory seems to have lost sight of both the individual and the spiritual. Why do hermits, for example, those who have abandoned society and all organizations, seek a relationship with the totally Other—God. After all, hermits, too, represent movements—though not in groups.

Furthermore, though deprivation theory is generally recognized as important in contributing to the rise of social movements, it does not explain a great number of other phenomena occurring in such movements: why some movements are highly nativistic, while others borrow heavily from other cultures; why deprivation in one area brings about a social movement, while the same type of deprivation in another area brings about no movement; why some movements are well organized while others loosely structured; why some movements are pacifistic while others turn to violence; why some are successful while others unsuccessful. And finally, the mechanism integrating the objective and the subjective has not been clearly defined (Gurney & Tierney, 1982).

Much of the anthropological and sociological theorizing about the rise of new movements has been in regard to societal systems—what happens when a larger society encroaches on a smaller, or what happens when material needs are not met by the system. As industrial societies seemed to have reached the ability to maintain prosperity through secularization without the aid of religious legitimation, it seemed that future discussion would focus less on the contribution of religion toward system integration and more on types of religions that have "no major functions for the entire society" (Fenn, 1972, p. 31).

## ALIENATION, DEPRIVATION, MODERNIZATION AND SECULARIZATION

L. L. Dawson (1998) rightly points out that much of the discussion regarding NRMs hinges on distinguishing between pre-modern and modern forms of social life. The discussion surrounding nativistic movements is largely made up of so-called premodern societies, while developed societies tend to be the ones labeled as modern. With modernization comes the secularization of established religion, driving people to sects and cults (Stark & Bainbridge, 1985) because overly secularized religion fails to provide satisfactory supernatural compensators.

Theories of alienation arising from modernization and secularization suggest that "acute and distinctively modern dislocation" produces alienation, anomie or deprivation (Robbins, 1988). The moral ambiguity of American culture, domination by bureaucracy, angst, the deinstitutionalization of the private realm and inexorable secularization were determined to be the origin of this dislocation.

Certain researchers (Chan, 2004; Lai, 2003; Leung, 2002; Thornton, 2002) have analyzed Falun Gong from the perspective of alienation and come to the conclusion that the Chinese in China have suffered alienation as a result of physical and psychological deprivation associated with modernization and commercialization. According to the theory, NRMs and socio-political movements are more likely to arise under these conditions—hence, the rise of Falun Gong. Such factors do indeed make sense in the China context, yet they do not explain why Falun Gong has spread among successful, well adjusted Chinese immigrants in a great number of foreign countries. Ownby (2003a), for example, rejected marginalization as a key factor among Falun Gong practitioners in the United States, based on his own fieldwork. Clearly, deprivation or alienation are, at best, only a partial explanation.

## RATIONAL CHOICE

A theory related to deprivation theory is rational choice theory (aka rational action theory), originally developed in microeconomics and political science. For their theory of religion, Stark and Bainbridge (1987) proposed that humans seek rewards and avoid costs. When rewards seemingly do not exist, they will tend to accept compensators—"I.O.U.s" (p. 37), especially when the reward cannot be had "in the here and now, by anyone" (Stark, 1997, p. 168). These compensators, promises of reward, are created by religious organizations, "social enterprises whose primary purpose is to create, maintain, and exchange supernaturally-based general compensators" (p. 42).

One strength of this theory is that it attempts to explain individual action and, at the same time, account for macro phenomena in societies. And it fits well within the established deprivation theory while attempting to account for spiritual beliefs and practices. A significant problem is that it does a poor job of explaining depression and suicide, which is found even among the rich and powerful, as if it were merely a way to limit the "net costs of future actions" (Stark & Bainbridge, 1987, p. 163). Clearly, such people have given up seeking the desired reward and compensators. Though Stark and Bainbridge might suggest that accepting death is compensation, disappointedly giving up is hardly an IOU form of compensation. Rational choice seems fundamentally materialistic at heart while seeking to explain immaterial phenomena, which are hard to explain as mere compensators (or promises)—such as actual healing, euphoria, and visions. It does not explain satisfaction gained in the present. These, too, are real reasons for which humans give up time, effort, money, fame, houses and lands.


## GLOBAL MOVEMENTS

Any discussion of movements spanning a number of countries must address a new phenomenon in the recorded history of the world—globalization. Most social scientists agree on five defining features of globalization:

1. the growing frequency, volume, and interconnectedness of movements of ideas, materials, goods, information, pollution, money and people across national boundaries and between regions of the world;
2. the growing capacity of information technologies to shorten or even abolish the distance in time and space between events and places in the world;

3. the diffusion of increasingly standardized practices and protocols for processing global flows of information, goods, money, and people;
4. the emergence of organizations, institutions and social movements for promoting, monitoring, or counteracting global forces, with or without the support of individual nation-states;
5. the emergence in particular countries or regions of distinctive or "local" ways of refracting the influence of global forces (Beckford, 2004, p. 254).

Roland Robertson (1992) identifies four major players in globalization: national societies, the system of societies, individuals, and humankind. These players feel the need to declare their identities as they become relativized by the other players. For example, religious groups or movements respond to unsettling global changes by urging a return to fundamentals, to identify humanity—not simply to return to what was, but to shape the world order. And as western countries are increasingly secularized, religious groups become marginalized.

The increased complexity and pluralism of the world scene makes solving problems of meaning especially difficult for anyone to claim much success. The human need for ultimate meaning remains. This desire is met through religions which are implicated in globalization through symbols of common humanity. Robertson suggests that a conventional understanding of economics and politics is inadequate for understanding movements because people need ultimate meaning and because world politics is fundamentally cultural. Religion, then, is important for understanding decisive social processes, both on a local and a global scale.

The most helpful theoretical designation in regard to the form of globalization exhibited by the Falun Gong is that it resembles a "Segmented Polycephalous [Ideological] Network (SP(I)N)" (Porter, 2003, p. 187). There are, however, problems with this designation. Falun Gong does resemble a SP(I)N in that the followers do network in multitudinous ways, and followers do take on leadership roles. However, they do so as facilitators or providers of technical expertise who tend to lack official or traceable structure. Further, Falun Gong is united in its doctrine (ideological). Yet Falun Gong has only one recognized head—Li Hongzhi—who is the only authority. Thus, Falun Gong is not really polycephalous.

## ADVANTAGES OF GLOBALIZATION

New movements benefit from globalization through new opportunities, encouragement, and even the impetus for pioneering applications of new technology (Beckford, 2004, p. 258). Examples include 16th century Protestant experiments with printing technologies, NRM use of the Internet, and Raelian experiments with human cloning. Beckford suggests that though NRMs have global aspirations, they have not gone beyond transnational. This is in part because NRMs remain marked by their particular cultural origins and their use of the Internet has more disadvantages—such as theft of their information—than advantages.

In this regard, Falun Gong is overwhelmingly Chinese in flavor, which may discourage non-Chinese. It has been shown, however, that about 10% of practitioners in North America are Westerners (Ownby, 2003a). Furthermore, the Falun Gong's use of the Internet is a major strategy for dissemination of Falun Gong theology and information regarding persecution. Indeed, the Falun Gong develops and maintains software for encrypting data and tunneling undetected through totalitarian firewalls, providing communication and access to any information and service on the Internet (Clearwisdom.net, 2004). It seems that Falun Gong has bypassed Beckford's limitations for NRMs.

Shupe (1991) suggests that the Soka Gakki are somewhere between a revitalization movement and a globalistic movement. Given the historical and cultural context, they are a revitalization, but they are a globalistic movement in that they have adapted their activities to a contemporary context, appealing to westerners and growing rapidly—approximately 33% per decade (L. L. Dawson, 2001).

Zablocki and Looney suggest that more research is needed as NRMs become "more global and more socio-movement-oriented" (2004, p. 314) in their approaches. They further suggest that some scholars of NRMs (Beckford, 2004; Bromley, 1998; Robbins, 1988, 2000) have tended to focus on the spiritual nature of NRMs while social movement scholars—such as (Gurney & Tierney, 1982; Hannigan, 1991; Lucas, 2004)—have tended to ignore the spiritual, focusing on external factors (politics, power, secularization, economic deprivation). Such dichotomizing between the spiritual and the natural is an artificial distinction. Some scholars (Robbins, Anthony, & Curtis, 1975) do take some account of spirituality as one of the four processes through which NRMs reintegrate adherents. Yet there is no concerted effort to account for the spiritual nature of movements, as distinguished from social interaction or social action. How do spiritual activities satisfy humans when they feel loss through modernization, relative deprivation, or secularization? Why is man a spiritual animal?

A second important change in research is that some scholars (Carter, 1990; L. Dawson, 2002; Lifton, 2000) are shifting from structural to process focused theories; instead of focusing on *why* questions, they are beginning to focus on *how* questions. One benefit of *how* questions is that they reveal how

NRMs "continuously create and maintain themselves" (Zablocki & Looney, 2004, p. 314).

A problem which has long been a concern and continues to mystify researchers is the profile for susceptibility to NRMs: Who is likely to convert to NRMs, and why do some leave the movements? Admitting that specifying a profile is difficult, L. L. Dawson, nevertheless, offers that memberships of "most NRMs are disproportionately young" (2003, p. 121). This, however, is not true of Falun Gong, which has been shown to appeal to a broad range of ages (Chan, 2004; Lowe, 2003), as well as to people of all levels of society (Schechter, 2001). The fact that in North America, Falun Gong practitioners tend to be well-heeled, and highly educated (Ownby, 2003a) can be easily explained, not by the nature of NRMs or even Falun Gong, but by the high bar set for immigration from China.

Listing the war on terrorism, insecure national identities, sophisticated anticult and countercult movements, and a decline in mainstream religions, Lucas (2004) predicts a dim future for NRMs and minority religions. He does not state clearly whether he expects that NRMs to be drastically reduced in number, eradicated, or whether there will simply be fewer freedoms and harsher crackdowns. Whatever the case, Lucas sees these trends driving toward a more secularized society.

## RELIGION

Though various social science theories do attempt to describe and explain new movements from an empirical and scientific perspective, few make any serious attempt to account for the seeming need in humans to engage in religion, as distinct from the social aspects of movements. Clearly, stresses, secularization, rational choice and relative deprivation cannot satisfactorily account for the proliferation and variety of religion in all cultures and social strata, never disappearing even during the "best of times." Why is man a "religious animal" (Burke, 2001, p. 152), as opposed to merely a "social being" (Aristotle, 2002,   p. 11)? Researchers and theorists engaged in the scientific study of religion have left such questions unexplored.

## BRAIN STUDIES

A whole new wave of research strategies in respect to attempting to address human religious tendencies is found in the field of brain studies. One notable experiment to explain man's religious tendencies was carried out using single photon emission computed tomography (SPECT) on a meditating Tibetan immersed in meditation (Newberg, D'Aquili, & Rause, 2001). They chose this instrument to show the brain during the height of meditation, when the subject feels a sense of timelessness, infinity and "connected to all of creation" (p. 4). The authors noted that the brain changed during meditation—the posterior superior parietal lobe, the part of the brain that orients humans in three dimensional space, relative to distance, direction and position. The brain does this by distinguishing between the individual and everything else. During meditation, the posterior superior parietal lobe stopped processing sensory input. Newberg, D'Aquili and Rause interpret this as the brain experiencing oneness with the cosmos. One critic, however, says that the brain "became essentially nonfunctional" (Pigliucci, 2004, p. 82), producing a delusion of oneness. Pigliucci reinterprets the data saying that "mystical experiences originate from the same neurological mechanisms that underlie hallucinations from sensorial deprivation and drug-induced 'visions'" (p. 83).

Perhaps both Newberg and Pigliucci are overly anxious to support their preconceptions. The feeling of oneness is not necessarily actual oneness. Nor is it sure that when the superior parietal lobe stops processing sensory input, it is nonfunctional, equal to sensory deprivation, and driving other parts of the brain to hallucinate. Since no attempt was made to deprive the subject of sensory input, the entire meditation process was internal, induced by the brain. The senses were still working. Could the reported experience of the subject and the SPECT data not be explained as focus? Perhaps more helpful conclusions could be drawn if the SPECT experiment were done on a larger population of religious practitioners during the height of their religious experience. Ultimately, the data can be interpreted within a scientific paradigm or a Buddhist paradigm, as well as others.

How might researchers and theorists escape their preconceptions? One anthropologist offers a new approach to the anthropology of religion. Klass (1995) criticizes social scientists for failing to define important terms and for failing to avoid explanations and methodologies that "carry judgmental baggage" (p. 6), for assuming that the ignorant and mentally deficient engage in silly practices that "lack instrumental validity and do not relate to objective reality" (p. 6). He suggests that social scientists might come up with better understandings if they did not judge the religious practices of others to be true, false, wise or stupid. In order to do this, neutral terms are needed—such as *animo*, from Esperanto, instead of *soul*. More importantly, he offers a careful definition of terms stripped of cultural bias, beginning with *religion*:

> that instituted process of interaction among the members of that society—and
> between them and the universe at large as they conceive it to be constituted—

which provides them with meaning, coherence, direction, unity, easement, and whatever degree of control over events they perceive as possible (p. 38).

A religion is concerned with:

Explanation, understanding, coherence; relief from psychological stress; release and channeling of emotions; social cohesiveness; sense of effectiveness and ability to cope with death, illness, and misfortune in general; maintenance of a sense of order by continual counteraction of powerlessness, randomness, meaninglessness, chaos (p. 38).

With these new formulations in mind, Klass proposes that the religious phenomena under investigation are "as 'true' and 'verifiable' as are *all* the things *we* do and believe in" (Klass, 1995, p. 6)—including science. If the practices did not have "sound ecological bases" (p. 6), people would ultimately abandon them.

The types of answers with which various thinkers have come up boil down to four: (a) God made us this way; (b) Man evolved this way for survival; (c) Man is a spiritual being as well as a material animal; (d) We can never know why, so get over it. The first, of course, is a statement of faith and cannot, therefore, be considered a scientific explanation. The second lacks proof, as the thoughts of prehistoric man left no fossil record; though evolution has been used as a trump card in favor of the scientific worldview since Darwin. The third cannot be proven in a laboratory, as spiritual is not quantifiable, though this has been tried (Newberg et al., 2001) with dubious conclusions. Nevertheless, comparative studies may provide evidence with which to form a theory. The fourth is merely accepting defeat in the face of a difficult problem and perhaps evidences an unwillingness to consider the possibility of other forms of knowing, aside from hard quantifiable matter.

Perhaps the most helpful anthropological studies to explain man's need for religion have been comparative studies of altered states of consciousness (ASC). For example, Winkelman (1986; 1997) points out that all societies have ASC associated with healing. He also suggests that ASC reflects normal brain function, that ASC provides "a basis for a more objective perception of the external world" (p. 404), and that it aids healing through "erasure of previously conditioned responses" (p. 406) and reprogramming of memories, including psychosomatic effects, that it can "ease memory blocks, to promote catharsis, and to shorten the course of therapy" (p. 407). Finally, Winkelman claims, based on Siegel's work (1989), that both animals and humans have an "innate drive to seek ASC" (p. 421) and that when the religious structures in society fail to meet these needs individuals will find a way to induce ASC, either through chemical or behavioral techniques.

There has been some research on movements using ASC. However, this research deals primarily with crowd manipulation and brainwashing—as in Scientology and est (Lindholm, 1992) or with the "western occult tradition" (York, 1995, p. 33)—not with movements arising in the Far East that have become global, nor, more importantly, with individuals who have specifically sought out movements to satisfy a personal, felt need that is not being met by existing structures in society.

## CONCLUSION TO LITERATURE REVIEW ON MOVEMENTS

The various theories offered to explain how and why man engages in movements and religious activities are helpful, but none of the theories explain all of the phenomena. Revitalization theory seems to be the most descriptive of the phases of movements, but lacks some of the specific causes and does not address why man is a religious animal. It seems, however, that each of the theories presented do address some feature(s) within the Falun Gong literature and the interviews I have conducted. The following section will discuss what various scholars have already said about Falun Gong and what remains to be addressed.

## SUMMARY OF THEORETICAL LITERATURE
## IN REGARD TO FALUN GONG

Of the literature reviewed, several researchers of Falun Gong implied a general acceptance of the theories surrounding new movements (Bell & Boas, 2003; Burgdoff, 2003; Irons, 2003; Lowe, 2003; Lu, 2005; S. J. Palmer, 2003; Porter, 2005). Observations, however, tend to highlight various features exhibited by Falun Gong, such as a charismatic leader (Burgdoff, 2003), the eclectic nature of Falun Gong theology (S. J. Palmer, 2003), secularization, deprivation and the global network of Falun Gong (Porter, 2005). Unfortunately, though these studies are excellent at describing the phenomena surrounding Falun Gong, they do not propose a unified theory.

Of special note, one researcher elaborates on how Falun Gong fits into revitalization theory (Ownby, 2000, 2003b) without ignoring deprivation and secularization, yet he does not discuss the globalized nature of Falun Gong. Nor does he, or any other researcher, attempt to incorporate what is known about ASC into the discussion. Yet the facility with which he fits secularization and deprivation into revitalization theory makes one wonder whether revitalization may also be able to absorb globalization and ASC. In short, a cohesive, all inclusive theory to explain Falun Gong has not been provided.

## SUMMARY OF CHAPTER 2

In this chapter, I reviewed the academic literature surrounding the rise of various types of movements (nativistic, revitalization, social, new religious, political and global), the factors contributing to the rise of such movements (colonization, secularization, deprivation, alienation, modernization, globalization, rational choice and, perhaps, altered states of consciousness), and the strengths and weaknesses of existing theories, which do not adequately account for all the phenomena surrounding Falun Gong. The next chapter discusses the research design behind the present study, which used grounded theory methodology to discover a unifying theory of how Falun Gong socializes its members.

*Chapter Three*

# Research Design and Methodology

In Chapter 1, I described the general background of Falun Gong and the reasons for studying the movement. In Chapter 2, I reviewed the literature related to new religious movements and discussed some of the areas needing development. In this chapter, I will provide an overview of the qualitative approach to research, with special attention to grounded theory methodology, which informs this study.

## QUALITATIVE RESEARCH

Qualitative research methodologies are widely accepted in the social sciences by those who seek to build theory, disaffirm hypothesis and construct transferable models (deMarrais & Lapan, 2004). While quantitative research merely tests for predetermined variables, qualitative research begins with the data, categorizing it by themes in order to discover variables. Of course, the variables found may have been reported elsewhere in the scholarly literature surrounding the topic. Often, however, new variables are found. One of the great strengths of qualitative research, therefore, is an ability to see phenomena afresh, seeing what has been previously overlooked. These variables may fit into existing theory, but sometimes, a new theory may be needed.

## GROUNDED THEORY METHODOLOGY

For this project, I chose Grounded Theory methodology (GT) because, unlike many other approaches to qualitative research, GT has a "systematic set of procedures to develop an inductively derived grounded theory about a phenomenon" (Corbin & Strauss, 1990, p. 24). The system includes seven key components:

1. A spiral of cycles of data collection, coding, analysis, writing, design, theoretical categorization, and data collection.
2. The constant comparative analysis of cases with each other and to *theoretical categories throughout each cycle.*
3. A *theoretical sampling process based upon categories developed from ongoing data analysis.*
4. The size of sample is determined by the '*theoretical saturation*' of categories rather than by the need for demographic 'representativeness,' or simply lack of 'additional information' from new cases.
5. The resulting *theory* is developed inductively from data rather than tested by data, although the developing theory is continuously refined and checked by data.
6. Codes 'emerge' from data and are not imposed *a priori* upon it.
7. The substantive and/or formal theory outlined in the final report takes into account all the variations in the data and conditions associated with these variations. The report is an *analytical product rather than a purely descriptive account. Theory development is the goal.*
   (Bryant & Charmaz, 2007, p. 154)

What makes GT unique and powerful is constant comparative analysis, theoretical saturation of categories and theoretical sampling. Data is compared to data throughout the study. The participants are compared; their statements are compared, and the categories generated are compared. Doing this clarifies for the researcher whether any new bit of data fits into existing categories or deserves a new category and whether more sources are necessary. If more sources are deemed necessary, the researcher chooses the sources by theoretical sampling—that is, choosing a source or asking a question because of its probable importance. When no new variables arise, a category is said to be saturated—hence, the term theoretical saturation of categories. Until that happens, the researcher continues to collect data from as varied a pool of sources as possible.

This study utilized the qualitative methodology of grounded theory (Corbin & Strauss, 1990; Strauss & Corbin, 1998). This approach allowed for exploration of the social processes present within the informal structure of the Falun Gong (Streubert & Carpenter, 1999). Analysis of the data collected was thus grounded, allowing emergence of a theory of how socialization takes place from the data and subsequent categories. Further hypotheses arose and were verified through interviews, observations and materials (Corbin & Strauss, 1990) published by those in the movement.

## DATA COLLECTION

The specific sources of data were of published FLG texts (articles, books and newspapers and web sites), open-ended interviews recorded in WMA format, and overt participant observation (Livesey, 2008).

Ten adults were interviewed—two from the US, two from Taiwan, five from Mainland China, and one from the Philippines. Of these, three were in their 30s, one in her 40s, two in their 50s, and four in their sixties. Six were males and four were females. Educational levels included two with high school diplomas, three with bachelor degrees, one in the process of finishing a PhD and four with PhDs. Professions included a hygienist, a nurse, two factory workers, a political consultant, three university professors/research-ers, one doctoral student, and one reporter. Seven of the participants spoke Mandarin Chinese as a native language, two English, and one Tagalog. Eight spoke fluent English, while the other two opted to give the interview primar-ily in Mandarin. What these numbers clearly showed was that those inter-viewed are drawn from a variety of demographic concerns—sex, age, cultural background, profession and education.

## VALIDATION STRATEGIES

In order to ensure internal validity (Creswell, 1998, 2003), several strategies were used:

1. Clarifying researcher bias. At the outset of the study, I noted potential bias. This is discussed below under the section "Role of the Researcher."
2. Triangulation of multiple sources. Ten different participants were inter-viewed at length, some multiple times. From these interviews, transcribed verbatim, arose the original themes. Phone and e-mail conversations were also conducted with participants. I also read extensively from the vast pool of published FLG materials (books, newspapers, flyers, programs, CDROMs, as well as Internet based media). Observations were recorded in Microsoft Word the same day as an encounter occurred. Themes from each source were constantly compared with themes from the other sources.
3. Member checks. Participants reviewed the open coding and axial coding categories to check my accuracy and interpretation. Further, after the first

draft of the study was completed, I e-mailed it to a key informant (who also passed it on to others) for feedback.

4. Peer debriefing. I shared my findings with a peer reviewer several times during the process of organizing and interpreting the data. The peer reviewer inspected my methodology, data and interpretation, as well as listened to my stories and my musings.

5. Audit trail. Besides keeping copies of all sources (such as interviews, notes, e-mails), I kept copies of the various stages of the data analysis process, from transcription to open coding and axial coding categories, indeed all the way through to the final model. An auditor could review the entire project.

## ROLE OF THE RESEARCHER

In GT, the researcher's role is to observe and interview. I was comfortable with this role because of my familiarity with Chinese culture, my intense curiosity about Falun Gong, and because of my own appreciation for spiritual and moral values. In the Introduction to this study, I told of my first encounter with a *qigong* practitioner in China. That was my second year in China. Since that time, I have continued to teach Chinese students in Asia and in the United States—though I have expanded my repertoire of subjects from English as a second language to English literature, composition, speed reading, critical thinking, education and cross-cultural studies. I speak Chinese, and my wife is Chinese.

My appreciation for moral and spiritual values stems from my being raised to be a fundamentalist Christian. Indeed, my parents were raised to be Pentecostal Christians, and they raised me in the same tradition. Though, today, I would describe myself as evangelical, a concern for truth, for moral foundations and for spirituality are ever with me. This appreciation for spiritual concerns has aided me in hearing what the participants were saying. I believe openness, along with objectivity, is necessary for successful data analysis.

In this study, I never felt that my own faith needed to be defended or that that of the practitioners should be justified. In this sense, this study falls into the category of what some have called compassionate ethnography. This study has not been about establishing the truth of Falun Gong but about discovering a theory of how Falun Gong educates. In order to do this, I have kept the perspective of Corbin and Strauss in mind: "all theoretical explanations, categories, hypotheses, and questions about the data . . . should be regarded as provisional . . . until they are found to fit this situation" (1990, p. 45).

## Ethical Considerations

Whenever interviewing is a primary method of data collection in a research study, ethical considerations must be addressed (Fontana & Frey, 1994). Therefore, before conducting any interviews or observations, I obtained approval from Biola University's Protection of Human Rights in Research Committee (PHRRC).

I protected the rights of the participants by first apprising them of my interest in doing an academic study of FLG and asked if they would be interested in giving me an interview. When they consented—indeed, everyone I approached did—I further explained that in order to protect their human rights, I was required to provide them with a consent form for them to sign (see Appendixes A and B), which included my contact information and that of Biola University, should they have any questions about (or problems with) the study.

Together, we went over the form, which explained how their participation was voluntary and that they could refuse to participate or discontinue their participation at any time without penalty or loss of benefits to which they might otherwise be entitled. And I assured them that their identity would be strictly confidential and that no personally identifying information would be released without their written consent.

Confidentiality was strictly maintained in this study by masking all personally identifiable information. The data corresponding with each participant was assigned a code number. Only I knew the identities of the participants, and only I and my research assistant (my wife) had access to the raw data collected because all transcripts, notes and recordings were kept in a locked file drawer in my office when not in use.

As far as could be reasonably determined, there were no overt risks to people participating in this study. No participants were members of "vulnerable populations" or subject to "undue influence." Participants were free to decline to answer or to withdraw from the study at any time. And, aside from the questionnaire (see Appendix C) which collected general statistical, census type data, only open-ended questions were used (see Appendixes D, E, F and G).

After I obtained signed, informed consent, each participant was interviewed by me and asked to describe his or her experience in Falun Gong. The interview was conducted in a place of the participant's choosing, such as the park, the participant's home, their office or a restaurant.

Finally, aside from the possible problems, participants were apprised of possible benefits of the research to themselves and to the public in general—in particular, making public the grounded theory of education in FLG.

## Falun Gong Texts

As the FLG provides their materials in freely downloadable electronic formats, besides traditional media, and in a variety of translations, this study focuses efforts on electronic English media, except for where discrepancies or problematic terms require consulting the Chinese electronic texts, or in the rare cases where English is not available. Relying on electronic formats is warranted because the materials are endorsed and provided by the FLG; the materials are quickly, easily and freely obtained; and they are well translated.

## Semi-Structured Interviews

I gained consent from practitioners before interviewing them. Practitioners were apprised of their rights and asked to sign consent forms in either English (see Appendix A) or Chinese (see Appendix B), depending on the preference of the practitioner. The interview began with the participant filling out a questionnaire (see Appendix C). Then I asked open-ended and semi-structured questions, either in English or in Mandarin Chinese (see Appendix D), depending on the preference of the participant. The reason for using open-ended questions was to allow the participant to respond as freely as possible, aiding me in avoiding dogmatic ties to any preconceived ideas or biases. The reason for maintaining a semi-structured format was (a) to allow the participant to address questions already raised, (b) to allow the participant to raise unexplored questions or problems, and (c) to allow the participant to elaborate on the emerging theory—aiding me in discovering it—while providing for an in-depth conversation to proceed as naturally as possible. As the grounded theory emerged, the questions were changed in order to confirm predicted responses and to develop the theory further (see Appendix E).

As the focus of the interviews changed from the individual's practice of Falun Gong to the nature of a Falun Gong school (the Ming Hui School), the questions were altered again to fit the role of the two participants in this phase of the interview process: a principal (see Appendix F) and a parent (see Appendix G).

Responses were recorded utilizing a digital voice recorder (Olympus WS-320M), after which the interviews were transcribed verbatim and analyzed. Interviews conducted in Mandarin Chinese were transcribed and translated by a native speaker of Mandarin Chinese and checked for accuracy by another native Mandarin Chinese speaker. Interviews conducted in English were transcribed by me. As none of the respondents objected to the use of a recording device, the researcher focused attention on the discussion and made field notes afterward. In a few cases, the notes were checked by the respondent for accuracy.

## Observations

For this study, overt participant observation (Livesey, 2008) was utilized. Overt participant observation is observation of the behavior of the participants in the study. The word *overt*, implies that the researcher is open with the group's members about the purpose, nature, scope, and duration of the research, and "the research is done with the permission and co-operation of the group" (para. 2). Further, the distinction between observer and participant is maintained as the role of the researcher is more on observing the participants' behavior than participating in the behavior. In this study, memos of observations were recorded by hand in the field and typed up later the same day.

## Setting and Sample

The setting for this study comprised several venues where FLG practitioners were either known to meet, or at meeting places of their choice. These included two public parks, a university campus, a private home, a restaurant and a place of business. These interview settings allowed for the possibility of the influence of context on different types of behavior or opinions.

## Participants

The participants interviewed were primarily of Chinese (People's Republic of China) extraction. Participants' referrals and suggestions aided the researcher, not only in discovering a theory, but in snowball sampling (Atkinson & Flint, 2004)—finding the most appropriate participants for subsequent interviews. I began recruitment by meeting practitioners at a public practice site (the locations of such sites are published on the Internet), making these prospective participants aware of the researcher's interest in doing a study of education in the FLG movement, and asking for interviews and referrals. This procedure aided in ensuring that the data collected were representative and accurate. Through these in-depth interviews of as many types of practitioner as possible, I aimed to understand the experiences of people within FLG, especially in regard to education and socialization. During this phase, the researcher also considered the participants' commitment level (such as core followers, ordinary followers and peripheral practitioners) as a helpful gage in determining how information gleaned fits into the overall picture.

## DATA ANALYSIS

Analysis of data proceeded based on accepted grounded theory methodology. First, it must be noted that the steps described below are not mutually exclusive, but overlap, sometimes taking place simultaneously. Furthermore, as grounded theory methodology requires constantly comparing data to data—the constant comparative method (Glaser & Strauss, 2006). The FLG texts were compared with the interviews and observations pursuant to answering research questions 1-4D and to developing a theory of education in FLG. This procedure helped to ensure accuracy, consistency and overall faithfulness to the data, and, hopefully, the subject being studied. Nevertheless, it must also be stated that the four relatively sequential processes in grounded theory data analysis were followed: open coding, axial coding, selective coding and portraying a conditional matrix.

In open coding, the researcher read the texts—in this case interviews (transcribed verbatim) and published FLG texts—for concepts, processes, emotions, or any content pertaining to the phenomenon under study. These were noted in the margin, as the researcher read the text line-by-line. Where possible, codes were adopted from the exact words from the respondent or text, called *in vivo* codes (Glaser & Strauss, 2006, p. 40). As open codes form categories, the researcher looked for subcategories (properties), which were placed on a continuum from one extreme to another.

In action (axial) coding, the researcher assembled the data to form a logic diagram (coding paradigm) that identified the causal conditions (conditions influencing the central phenomenon), specific strategies (actions resulting from the central phenomenon), intervening conditions (conditions that influence the strategies) and described the consequences of the strategies for the central phenomenon.

In selective coding, the researcher identified the story that integrated the categories in the axial coding model. At this time, the conditional propositions (hypotheses) were presented.

Finally, the researcher provided a conditional matrix explaining the conditions that influence the central phenomenon.

Throughout the process of coding, sorting and writing, the researcher used "theoretical memoing" (Glaser, 1978, p. 89) to record ideas about the data as a way of elaborating on the developing analytical categories. This memo writing began the task of writing the research report.

## DELIMITATIONS

This study was confined to practitioners of Falun Gong in the Los Angeles area and to published media to which practitioners have access. Many of my participants came into the study through referrals. One practitioner was so busy with his job that finding a mutually acceptable time was virtually impossible.

This study was limited to studying the process of socialization as education in Falun Gong. Unlike some qualitative methodologies, in Grounded Theory methodology, not all data is equally significant. Data collection and analysis was subject to theoretical sampling, theoretical saturation of categories and constant comparative analysis.


## LIMITATIONS

From a theoretical standpoint, the findings of this grounded theory study may not be generalizable to other movements because of the nature of the historical/cultural/religious background from which FLG springs. Most notably, none of the various Daoist "schools" throughout the 5,000-year history of Chinese civilization has ever had a formal educational structure; Daoism has always been informal. The same can be said of the White Lotus sects, though it is not true of Buddhism, which has a well documented history of formal education. In contrast, other advanced civilizations from which movements arise have had formal educational systems. Movements arising from nativistic cultures have not shown any evidence of becoming globalized. Although the results of this study provide an explanation only for the experience of the FLG in Southern California, the emergent theory may aid in the revision of movement theory in general—especially for this globalized, information age.


## SUMMARY OF CHAPTER 3

This chapter discussed the research design behind the present study, which used grounded theory methodology to discover a unifying theory of how Falun Gong in Southern California socializes its members. The next chapter presents the themes that arose from the interviews conducted.

# Chapter Four

# Results: Socialization
# per the Interviews

The central phenomenon under investigation in this grounded theory study is the process of socialization, driven by conversion (adopting the new worldview) and growth (developing or reaching higher levels of maturity). The term *conversion*, however, is somewhat problematic. A few practitioners objected to the term conversion because it has a "negative" connotation, especially in Chinese. To some, conversion implies that the practitioner has given up one religion for another. In reality, many practitioners were atheists before embracing FLG. To others, conversion implies that FLG is a religion or that there is some rite of passage in becoming a practitioner. Practitioners, however, are dissatisfied with designating FLG as a religion. They point out that FLG affects every area of life. There is no rite of passage, no demarcation line or point at which one clearly stops being what one was and transforms into a practitioner.

One practitioner, an editor for *The Epoch Times*, suggested using the words *change, awareness* or *enlightenment*. Indeed, change is what I intend by the use of the word *conversion*, but change is too common a word, implying nothing of a worldview shift. The other words, *awareness* and *enlightenment*, imply cognition and, perhaps, a religious experience, but carry no sense of the group or of the movement in general. In this study, therefore, conversion does not imply any particular starting place. Nor does it designate FLG as a religion. It implies a process of change, a new sense of awareness, a feeling of enlightenment, in short, the process of becoming a FLG practitioner. There is no ceremony or dramatic event demarking a clear point at which someone stops being what one was and begins being a practitioner. It is a process controlled by one's own decisions—what one practices, what one understands and what one accepts as true. One practitioner put it this way, "We don't have a registration or anything. If you think you are, you are. If you think you are not, you are not." The gatekeeper is oneself.

Yet it must be understood at the outset of this chapter that many of the processes underlying both conversion and growth are the same, from choosing to listen as someone shares, choosing to do the exercises and meditation, or choosing to participate in any number of community experiences—such as the local groups, the large groups, or the Internet. Furthermore, many of the problems, topics and activities of the early stages of contact with FLG continue to drive socialization in an upward spiral of development.


## CONVERSION AND GROWTH

Practitioners decide to practice FLG largely as a choice after weighing the merits of this new movement. Convincing proofs include the following: a sense of fate, realization that persecution is taking place, appreciation of volunteerism, impact of shared stories, hope of improvement in personal health, and discovery of a more satisfying vision.

The ways in which these convincing proofs are communicated to prospective practitioners include a variety of truth-telling strategies, such as visibility in public parks where practitioners do exercises; face to face communication; print media; analogue technologies (e.g. telephone, shortwave radio); global digital networks; volunteerism; experience sharing sessions; shows and demonstrations; and digital guerilla activity. These same forms of truth-telling continue during the growth process.

Growth is seen as an individual becomes aware of the truth of FLG. His/her character is also developing. Character is connected to morals, culture, bodily health and spiritual level. The improvement of one's character is obtained through reading the *Zhuan Falun*, doing the five exercises, and in keeping the principles of the universe—truth, compassion and tolerance (真, zhēn; 善, shàn; 忍, rěn)—as the standard for appropriate thought and action.


## TRUTH, COMPASSION AND TOLERANCE

A recurring theme that arose out of the interviews was that the nature of the universe is truth, compassion and tolerance and that aligning oneself with this nature is beneficial. In eight out of the ten interviews, this three-word concept figured as a major theme, being mentioned and explained. In the two interviews where this phrase did not occur, one of the practitioners could be described as committed, but at a lower developmental stage, admittedly not completely understanding the doctrine. He says, "I'm reading the book and, and I'm reading it every time I have time. It's hard to understand. Some of this terminology I don't understand." The other a practitioner's comments were much more focused on how FLG combats communism than on its philosophical nature. Yet he did distinguish FLG practitioners from other humans this way: "Body the same, mind's different," thus indicating that the mindset of FLG practitioners is different from that of other people.

Every element of FLG thought and practice can be traced to this theme. Pursuing truthfulness, compassion and tolerance is the philosophy, the *modus operandi*, the filter through which all decisions are to be made, including how one interacts with others and how one manages one's thoughts. One longtime practitioner explained it this way:

> Well, we just actually cultivate on every issues. I mean, it's hard to say, easily. Now you get to a new level, but by making progress on each issue, you're basically improving. For example, like we all, the principle we always try to stick to is to be Truthfulness, Compassion and Tolerance. So for example, to me to be honest, truthful, it's easy. For example, I say, you have mistake. I say, "I tell you, David, you have a mistake, you should correct it." That's truthful. But am I compassionate? Not necessarily. Because, for example, I may tell you, "oh, you should do that," but subconsciously I think I'm correct, or maybe I see these things more clearly, I'm righter than you are. So in that case, to us it's not compassionate. So you should really be compassionate, you know, and people will be touched. It's not like … so many times when you point out an honest mistake and you feel resistance, why? Because you're not so compassionate. You're right, but I just don't want to accept that. [laughs] So it's difficult. Another, like tolerance, it's not like, oh, I try to be tolerant to you. For example, the first time, like, a someone say bad words about me. How should I do? As a practitioner, you should be, "Oh, OK. I don't care. OK, that's one thing. Another thing, is that you should look inward, "Oh, why did he say bad things about me? Did I do something wrong?" You need to search inside and then really correct that. And then many people sometimes, you are really sad then you have tears on your face, "oh, they wrong me! They treat me wrong, OK? I don't want to explain but I still feel I'm wronged. You know? That's still not good because a practitioner, tolerant, you basically, even, still feel peaceful. You even don't feel sad that people treat you bad.

In summary, if one is unsure of whether or not he should point out someone's fault, he should ask himself if it is true that there is a fault. He should also evaluate whether or not it would be compassionate to point out the fault and whether or not his desire to do so is evidence of intolerance. Truthfulness, compassion and tolerance, thus, must be understood and applied together as a gestalt. Yet it is most visible in the various forms of truth-telling exhibited by FLG practitioners.


## Five Exercises

One of the most visible and distinctive features of FLG which arose as a common theme in the interviews is the five exercises that practitioners perform daily in public, usually in parks. All of the practitioners interviewed do the exercises, though not all of them elaborated on the exercises during the open-ended interviews. Nevertheless, all 10 either mentioned them directly or referred to them indirectly.

Aside from the fact that the exercises are purported to improve health and spiritual wellbeing and that doing the exercises in groups in public parks is purported to be even more effective than doing them alone or indoors, these exercises also have a socializing influence. For example, one practitioner told of a woman from Czechoslovakia who was visiting the United States. This woman decided to try out FLG after seeing the group practicing in the park. Before returning to her home country, she informed the group that she was going to take FLG back to Czechoslovakia to form a group. In short, when passersby notice practitioners doing the exercises in the park, some will embrace it. This example is not only one of socialization, but more specifically, of conversion.

Another theme of socialization which arises when discussing the exercises in the park is developmental growth. According to several of the participants, in both Buddhist and Daoist practice, meditation is done in private, or even as a hermit. But in FLG, the exercises are meditative, especially the fifth one, and are best done in public. One practitioner, who was from Taiwan, explained the benefit of practicing in public this way:

> If you hide in a mountain, hide in a cave, it may take you 1000 years. But the accomplish may still be less than the person who does one year in this world. Yeah, because, how you move up, you need some challenge, right? Somebody hit you, automatically, you get angry, that's attachment there, right? You hide in the mountain, nobody kick you, right? You don't get angry, so you don't move up. Every time you got the challenge you, you succeed in that, you move up. You get rid of attachment. Yeah, but the guy hide in the mountain, nobody challenge him, his attachment is still there.

Similarly, a veteran practitioner from PRC noted how harassment from society benefits the practitioner: "That's why earth is a good place because in this society a lot of people will give you a chance to get rid of your attachments."

## Volunteerism

A theme that runs throughout is that learning FLG is free. Anyone who instructs is a volunteer—even at New Tang Dynasty Television and at the Ming Hui School. Several practitioners pointed out this FLG policy of always volunteering their services for free. This is clearly appealing as the only loss is the time, an hour or so spent in giving FLG a try.

## Sharing

Practitioners tend to be quite willing to share their experiences with anyone who will listen. Of all the practitioners I approached, not one refused to share. In fact, when I asked, "How has this interview been for you?" every single one thanked me for the opportunity to share. However, not all practitioners I approached were asked to participate in the study because of either time constraints or the nature of the delimitations of this study. For example, many of my participants came into the study through referrals. One practitioner was so busy with his job that finding a mutually acceptable time was virtually impossible. This study is limited to southern California. Another contact turned out to be no longer in southern California, but in New York. Nevertheless, they were all willing.

The most visible form of sharing is on the street, at the airport or at the Chinese embassy. Yet though this form seems common, only two of the ten participants came to FLG through such sharing.

## Conversion Stories

Perhaps the most strikingly effective methodological activity that practitioners engage in is telling conversion stories. When I asked practitioners how they became involved in FLG, they all told their story, which included stories from other practitioners that had influenced their decision to try FLG. Not one practitioner replied with a series of points or logic, such as one might find among Christians who came to faith through being presented with the Four Spiritual Laws (Bright, 1993)—an evangelization strategy presenting four points leading up to the sinner's prayer: God loves you; you are separated from God by your sin; Jesus Christ died to pay for your sin; you must pray and accept Jesus Christ as Savior and Lord.

Every conversion story included themes of persecution, healing, and a search for meaning in life. Those most influenced by persecution stories were those who were already active in demonstrations against human rights abuses. For example, one American practitioner had previously been involved in demonstrations against human rights abuses in El Salvador and alongside

Native Americans in the United States. Another Chinese practitioner from PRC had been previously involved in fighting against human rights abuses in the communist state.

Another driving force in conversion stories is a search for the meaning of life. Converts to FLG often have prior experience in other movements, such as Christianity, Alcoholics Anonymous, New Age, Hinduism, Buddhism, or Daoism. It is not so much that these converts had been disillusioned with the other movements but that FLG seemed to offer a better overall experience and/or explanation. Comments such as, "this is the best"; FLG could "explain everything"; "Falun Gong is so good"; "I just feel good. That's good enough!"; "Today's a fantastic place where I am, right today. Today I've got money. I've got good health. I'm more happy than I've ever been. And I'm much more wiser. Ah, to me, that's a win-win." In terms of story, it is a happy ending.

The third feature of conversion is the inclusion of stories they had heard from FLG practitioners touting the health benefits of FLG. These stories of dramatically improved health were influential in conversion decisions, as evidenced by the fact that stories of healing were worth retelling, second hand, when relating their own conversion stories. For some, healing was a primary motivating factor. These practitioners had been searching for a cure for illness, not the meaning of life. Yet the effectiveness of FLG for healing gave credence to the overall FLG worldview.

In short, depending on the background of the individual, one of the three themes may take preeminence over the other two, but all three themes are present in each conversion story.

## Individual and Group Sharing

As noted above, sharing is done regularly in small groups. Aside from any impact it may have in the process of conversion, its primary purpose is to enhance growth in terms of development, becoming a better practitioner, reaching higher developmental levels. Developmental growth occurs mostly as a result of the shared experiences, whether insights or stories.

Though sharing may be done at any time through the myriad ways in which humans network, sharing is built into FLG practice in regular "sharing sessions." Local groups usually have a weekly sharing session which lasts an hour or two. During sharing sessions, practitioners will read from *Zhuan Falun*, and discuss their insights and experiences. As every part of life is ultimately related to the practitioner's cultivation practice, the experiences shared tend to be the practical application of truth, taken from daily life and related back to *Zhuan Falun*. The most common feature of this sharing is the success story.

The largest type of sharing session, an FLG conference, occurs somewhere in the world virtually every month. As conferences were not elaborated on in the interviews, this will be discussed further in the chapter on FLG publications.

## Demonstrations, Parades and Shows

More dramatic ways of telling the truth include group activities that are more likely to draw public attention: demonstrations outside the Chinese consulate, parades, and shows. One practitioner from Taiwan admits that he does not take part in demonstrations—not out of fear or disagreement with the philosophy, but because of his attachment to his wife, who does not approve of his participation in FLG. This does not keep him from practicing in the park, though. Another practitioner—part Native American and part Jewish—does participate in demonstrations, not only in Southern California, but has gone with other American FLG members into Mexico to demonstrate.

A related form of demonstration is the parade, where participants in this study admit to passing out fliers. Though consulates are political entities by nature, parades—in the US at least—are American cultural celebrations. FLG participation focuses on the human rights abuses of the PRC government. While the effectiveness of this method may be marginal, practitioners continue telling the truth with their characteristic high standards of morality. One practitioner comments on how he cleans up afterward:

> Not something just, you know, you give them, here, hi, hi, hi, and you walk down and you come back and you find them on the ground, people throw it away. You know, like a couple of parades..... Then when we come back, we're picking them up, you know.

Shows are a unique platform for promoting FLG, human rights and traditional Chinese culture. One practitioner introduces it thus:

> I think you may heard that we Falun Gong are organizing in the past few years, a Chinese show, called "The Chinese New Year Gala." And its, all of them are Chinese dancing, singing, all these things, which made the Chinese government so threatened....You see, all the traditional Chinese drama, you know, no matter how skillful they are, the whole story always tell people how to behave. You know, when you see all these colorful dress, all the amazing singing, all these things, and finally you even moved to tears, and finally you realize through the whole drama how to behave. That's essence . . . exactly. Think like the spirit of the show. In nowadays, China, sometimes they say, that's a traditional Chinese show but they just put the same dress without the soul....That's not traditional Chinese culture.

It is this so-called *soul* that the Chinese government finds problematic. Instead of the Chinese Communist Party monopolizing the discussion on Chinese culture and tradition, an entity completely outside of party control (the FLG) has its own soapbox—and sells tickets. Another practitioner explains how the idea for a show gets its startup money: "the people who run the show will pay for it, the cost." Meanwhile, "the Chinese consulate here in Los Angeles," "call[s] all the sponsors of our show to withdraw their sponsorship."

## Print and Sharing

Print media have a significant role in sharing in FLG. Pamphlets, posters, newspapers and books all are used in hopes of drawing individuals to consider the claims of FLG. Among the participants of this study, none referred to posters as an influential element in their initial contact or original decision making processes. However, pamphlets, newspapers and books are all mentioned. The most mentioned of the print media regarding decisions to try FLG was the central text of the movement—*Zhuan Falun*. Though it does not appear as the initial contact tool, it does appear early in all of the practitioners' conversion accounts.

## Books and Sharing

One practitioner had read *China Falun Gong* before *Zhuan Falun* was out. She liked both books and continued to read them, even without following FLG. She and her sister "both loved it." When *Zhuan Falun* was finally published, she said it was "the best book I've ever read." Another practitioner had originally been curious about *Zhuan Falun*, the banned religious book. After she read it, she thought it was "the most powerful" of any religious book she had read. It could "explain everything…the universe…all the human being, everything can explain very clear. So I believe the *Zhuan Falun*." She came to the conclusion that it was written by "something like a god, something like a Buddha."

## Books and Growth

As noted earlier, conversion and growth overlap. This is seen in the various ways different types of technology support growth. For example, the *Zhuan Falun* is not only for conversion, it serves as an all-purpose source of truth and inspiration. One practitioner described studying *Zhuan Falun* as "getting more education, more education." As a result, he can now listen to friends, instead of being the center of attention. Another practitioner referred to *Zhuan*

*Falun* as a more systematic teaching. Most read the book together with their group members at least once a week, aside from their personal reading time.

Practitioners often refer to *Zhuan Falun* as "The Book," as if there is no other text that deserves such a designation. For example, one practitioner recounts how a terminally ill lady swore off all western medicine, saying, "'the book says, 'don't think of the disease, just forget about it'"—and she was soon healed. The book is a source of information about the practitioner's relationship to the master. For example, one practitioner says, "in the book, said, 'I give you the Falun.'" Another says, "I feel Master will be there through the Book." The book is the source of solutions: "Sometimes I have questions. And then I would pick up the book, and I would just open it. And then I would read and then here's the answer."

*Zhuan Falun* is the primary source of a new worldview and culture. One American practitioner explains, "it's completely different from the way I was taught [before FLG]." *Zhuan Falun* is the primary textbook, even for children. The principal of the Ming Hui School said, the children "have to study Fa, that is study of *Zhuan Falun*.

## Newspapers

Practitioners of FLG recognize the importance of newspapers in presenting the news from an FLG perspective. Two different practitioners—one a regional coordinator and another a research scientist—brought up *The Epoch Times* in discussion, to make sure I was aware of this "pro-Falun Gong" newspaper. The scientist pointed out that *The Epoch Times* is "pretty much, everywhere in the world, except mainland China. But actually, last year, somebody broke in and beat the people there....they didn't take money...they took his notebook you know." This documented case (Poole, 2006), presumably an attack by PRC henchmen, shows how politicized FLG has become, regardless of whether FLG is motivated more by politics or by spiritual concerns.

Nevertheless, though the FLG would see *The Epoch Times* simply as a way to tell the truth, the government of China would see much of what *The Epoch Times* reports as sedition. For example, the regional coordinator asked me if I had read the *Nine Commentaries on the Communist Party*. At the time, I had not. Upon asking who the author was, the participant replied that it was written by *The Epoch Times* editors. The *Nine Commentaries* are "about the whole history of communism," and about "the strategy they have been using" and about "how people are fooled." These commentaries give examples of how communism, which is "from Russia and Germany," has been "systematically destroying the Chinese traditional culture."

Of course, this critique is rejected by the government. In fact, the *Nine Commentaries* are "forbidden in China for anyone to read it. Even the policemen are not supposed to because anyone who reads the article will immediately know what communism is." Nevertheless, the *Nine Commentaries* are available everywhere through nontraditional means, as noted in the section on the Internet below.

## Telephones

Besides the printed text, there are other ways in which truthfulness, compassion and tolerance can be advanced. For example, the telephone is mentioned by several practitioners in reference to conversion and growth. One American became a practitioner as a result of a wrong number. Despite the wrong number, a relationship began which brought about a new practitioner. One woman from China was curious about FLG. When she was told that a man in her class was a practitioner, she asked him about *Zhuan Falun*. Then he gave her "his telephone number" and soon passed on a copy of the book to her.

Aside from sharing, the telephone is a standard communication tool for mobilization. It was telephone communication that enabled so many people to mobilize on Zhongnanhai. Commenting on that event, one LA practitioner told me, "They're from the whole country, different area. Phone call, you coming tomorrow." In short, the interviews show the FLG practitioners using the telephone in two ways: to share with others and to inform the group. At times, FLG use of the telephone bears resemblance to cold calling or telemarketing. Indeed, in Chapter 5, telephone socialization themes are discussed in greater detail.

Phones are also used for maintenance of relationships and mutual encouragement. For example, when one LA area practitioner returned to China for a visit, she called the friend who originally introduced her to FLG. What practitioners say over the phone in China must be circumspect, especially if one is in hiding from the government, "because the phone could be bugged." So her friend did not reveal her location over the phone.

The ubiquity of cell phones in American society can be a hindrance to practicing truthfulness, compassion and tolerance. Hence, ignoring the phone is sometimes a preferred strategy. For example, one American practitioner who was new to FLG was surprised by the following experience:

One of the Falun Gong people that I was with Sunday, he had that phone, so we were talking, and he says, "Oh, excuse me" and closes his phone. And I say, "Why?" And he said, "Well, I'm talking to you, and I want to hear you."

## E-mail

E-mail figures prominently as an important tool of FLG. For example, one practitioner's conversion to FLG begins with an e-mail. A friend at Harvard University had recently converted to FLG and she e-mailed all of her Chinese friends at Caltech so they would know of her wonderful discovery. Another way practitioners use e-mail is to share information. A practitioner in LA told me that FLG was able to mobilize so many people for the protest at Zhongnanhai was e-mail. In short, the interviews show the FLG practitioners using e-mail in two ways: to share with non-practitioners or to inform the group. Yet it must be understood that this is not in the context of canvassing or spamming. No such activity has been noted anywhere in this study. Rather, the spreading of FLG messages in e-mail is for the benefit of family and friends.

## The Internet

The Internet, according to the interviews, plays an integral part in the lives of practitioners. For example, though the interview questions were open-ended and did not mention any form of media, eight out of the ten practitioners brought up their own Internet use. Two discussed use of the Internet in their search for a more satisfying religious experience. One used the Internet to find someone to teach him FLG: "they had the website where we could go, so I got on the computer and what popped up was Irvine." In five of the cases, news of FLG piqued their interest just prior to conversion. Four brought it up as being instrumental to their own conversion. In one case, the fact that FLG was being persecuted in China made her look again at the *Zhuan Falun*, which she had read before. One practitioner explained how she taught her aging mother, who craved world news, to circumvent the government's firewall. She "checked the Internet" and exclaimed, "Oh, there's software can do that. I said, 'OK, try it.'" The mother later became a FLG practitioner. In short, the Internet plays an integral role in conversion through providing news of the practice, news of the persecution, and a broad avenue for sharing anywhere in the world.

The role of technology in supporting growth is seen in how the Internet is a source through which individuals become aware of the movement. It also provides the individual with a vast array of information about FLG. Once an individual becomes interested, an early step in the socialization process is obtaining a copy of *Zhuan Falun*. Often a practitioner will lend a copy to an interested individual. One participant was initially lent a downloaded copy of *Zhuan Falun*. Or the individual simply downloads a free copy in the language of his/her choice. Later, most buy a traditionally published copy, either through the Internet or from a local store. One practitioner was told, "oh, just keep it [the downloaded copy], until I getting the real book from the store."

As FLG has many practitioners all over the world but only one Master, the Internet provides a quick and easy way for much teaching and learning to take place. According to one participant, on the Internet, Master Li provides "a lot of different lectures, so actually explained it—more detailed explanation—on top of *Zhuan Falun*. Or some more specific help to answer the question." In fact, because of the FLG software for circumventing firewalls in totalitarian countries, "you can read anything you want. . . . . Everyone loves it." Though the Chinese government "spends big money to block this software," a new version will soon be released that works.

Similarly, as in the case of one practitioner interviewed, it is often through the Internet— from an article on an FLG website—that followers become aware of the existence of the Ming Hui school, a weekend school for practitioners' children to learn Chinese language and culture and, of course, FLG.

## Secular Media

Another educational strategy that FLG uses is television. Participants in this study discussed television, both in reaction to what the Chinese government has done and in terms of FLG response. For example, on January 23, 2001, a group of individuals set themselves on fire in Tiananmen Square in Beijing. Within hours, Xinhua news agency, controlled by the Chinese government, reported the incident on nationwide television as promulgated by Falun Gong practitioners. This suicide controversy, which first arose on Chinese television, has become an important piece of ammunition for FLG. One practitioner analyzes what the Chinese government did, "That [Tiananmen self-burning] is staged by the government. They, they use the television, to you know, some protective the clothes, those, mask, that is not real."

## FLG Media

Furthermore, not only does FLG address this particular controversy orally but also in a number of technologies (such as web pages, video CDs and pamphlets and newspapers). They don't stop there, but they broadcast the message as well. In fact, the establishment of a pro-FLG television station—New Tang Dynasty Television (NTDTV)—could be considered a platform, not only for responding to threats to the movement, but for further dissemination of the FLG vision—a significant *coup d'état*. One Chinese practitioner who was there at the beginning of NTDTV describes its establishment, going from an idea to global broadcasting via satellite in only five years:

First only three guys, three guys…on a garage…. All the people donation to make it. Only few years. Few years. I know the television, New Dynasty Television, only five years, then they got four piece the satellite, of the global, 24 hours broadcasting.

## Interconnected Technologies

This last point, the use of satellites for global communication, is important in several ways. First, FLG practitioners plan strategically to ensure that the message of truthfulness, compassion and tolerance can be heard all over the world. Second, it illustrates the interconnectedness of the various electronic media. E-mail is part of the Internet; television is now not merely broadcast via the airwaves but over the Internet and via satellite. Third, a reference to the Internet or to satellite could imply any number of technologies that support worldwide, textual, audio, visual and interactive content.

## MING HUI SCHOOL

The name for the Ming Hui School comes from the words 明 *ming* and 慧 *huì*. Ming carries the concepts of clear, bright, understanding; and hui means intelligent. The FLG literature translates the phrase *minghuì* as "pure insight" or "clear wisdom."

## Parents

I was first introduced to the concept of the Ming Hui School by a Chinese immigrant practitioner whose teenage daughter also practices FLG. The mother discovered the Ming Hui School on a FLG website. According to her the Ming Hui School meets "in every city, like Los Angeles, we have only Saturday afternoon." At present, the Ming Hui School offers instruction only on Saturday from 2 p.m. to 8 p.m., but may be planning to offer classes throughout the week. The approach is a curriculum for children that includes "the arts, they training the those young people, young kids from very young." She mentioned dance, singing, and musical instruments. Unfortunately, she could provide little information as she lived too far away from the school to send her daughter there. At this point, I determined to find a parent whose child was attending the Ming Hui School. A few inquiries produced a friend of a friend—a method of meeting people that is at once both quintessentially Chinese and FLG.

It seems that there is little deliberation for parents in deciding to send their children to the Ming Hui School. The parent introduced to me described how she decided to send her child to the school: "When I found out there is a Ming

Hui school, you know, and sure there is a chance, then we go." In this case, the husband does not practice FLG. He is from a former communist country in Europe. The mother, however, is from China and practices FLG. Yet he apparently does not mind that his wife and child practice FLG. She says, "He is happy." When asked what benefit the parent hopes the child will gain—such as the Chinese language—she replied, "Language and like to learn Falun Gong, both." So for her, the motivation for sending her child to the Ming Hui School is rooted in instilling Chinese culture and passing on FLG to one's children. It should also be noted that, based on earlier interviews and the emerging model of socialization, I expected this response. So the parental category was saturated.

## The Principal

The next step in discovering the Ming Hui School approach to socialization was to interview the principal, a connection easily made. The questions for this interview were not so much about the experience of the principal in learning and practicing FLG as about what Ming Hui School is, who it serves and what it teaches and how.

As the other practitioners had intimated, Ming Hui School is basically a weekend school to teach the children of practitioners FLG and traditional Chinese culture. And though the school is not currently registered with the government, there is concern for providing legitimate education. For example, the principal offered, "our teachers are all volunteering willingly, but our teachers all have teaching certificate, the license." In fact, she later asked me if I knew where to find information on how private schools can register with the government of California.

Conversion to FLG does not seem to be a focus. Presumably, the children of practitioners are already positively predisposed toward FLG. Indeed, the primary goal of education at the Ming Hui School is to aid the children in the development of their temperament or disposition (from 心性 *xīn xìng*; 心 meaning heart, mind, intelligence or soul; 性 meaning nature or character) and bodily health. According to the principal of the Ming Hui School, through practicing FLG, the children's temperament

> can change, ascend up, and do mainly according to truth, compassion, and tolerance. As for practicing, *gōng*, is for their body and physical to change. It doesn't matter whether adults or children, they all would gain health for their body first, then as you practice *gōng*, you would improve your temperament, your body would change.

In the above quotation, the word *gōng* (功) is literally *work*. However, in this context, *gōng* is, according to one practitioner "a form of energy, with fine grains, much finer than *qì*. It's a higher, more powerful form of energy than *qì*, which is only something at the surface level." The practitioner causes *gōng* to spiral around the body and above the head in a column that transforms the body and mind to a higher level of existence. Further, the word *ascend* is a phrase in Chinese (昇華上來, *shēng huá shàng lái*) implying that the student's body and mind reach higher levels of development through practicing truthfulness, compassion and tolerance.

Aside from aiding the children, and by extension, the parents, another goal of the Ming Hui School is to recruit more students. The principal explains the reasons for the school's small size as lack of funding and failure to recruit:

> We have about over ten students. Mainly all are . . . the Falun Gong practitioners' children. Because we haven't . . . recruit student publicly . . . regular . . . regular students. Because we mainly . . . we don't have any funds, also the place is small. So we haven't recruit any other students.

Nevertheless, though they do not currently recruit, the principal does expect to do so in the future after the financial and classroom problems have been resolved. This is not simply a desire for the school to flourish, but for the Ming Hui School to be able to offer something unique to society. Indeed, concern for society is a recurring theme in FLG. The more people practicing FLG, the better society will be. The Ming Hui School principal touches on both of these issues in the following statement:

> The goals of school, actually we are hoping that later…oh…we can recruit more students. That is, I think what we want to do is…it's a very good thing for all the people. Because what we ask is truth, compassion, and tolerance, so…oh…but as of right now as you have know a lot about . . . we are lacking a lot of funding. That is our facil . . . our classroom problem and others. So we can't recruit students right now. But I think besides asking our current students to be able to reach truth, compassion, and tolerance, if we can recruit more students widely, I think, that is…is a very good thing for the society.

Again, the perceived need for growth is a driving force rooted in FLG ideology, as the following passage illustrates. For though this is a local Ming Hui School, the concern for the larger society extends far beyond Southern California to the United States, and even to the whole world:

> Falun Gong is good and beneficial for each and every country, right? Every one [FLG practitioner] is a good person, and all has healthy body. It's mainly because… I think you have met have met many people, you have interviewed many people. So you know that we are willing…to speak out about this. That

is if we all do as according to this, then this country, this society would all be a very good one.

## The Ming Hui Complementary Curriculum

The approach to socialization in the Ming Hui School is similar to what takes place among adult practitioners in that it includes the five exercises and experience sharing which aid in transformation of character. However there are significant differences. For example, it must be noted that the students' introduction to FLG does not occur as a result of dissatisfaction with their own health or existing culture, nor does it result of coming across a demonstration or being handed a pamphlet. Rather, children are predisposed toward FLG because of their parents. It is the parents who make the Ming Hui School an option for their children because they perceive a need for the inculcation of Chinese language and culture, as well as instruction in FLG. Thus, education in the Ming Hui School is geared to the needs of the student.

The way Chinese language and culture are taught in the Ming Hui School can be described as a student-centered approach, with attention to the best of the Chinese cultural tradition. An example of the student-centered approach is that the one student from a mixed marriage receives special attention. In this regard, the mother says, the teachers "give [my child], you know, more instruction or even speak English to him, to make sure he understands."

The student-centered approach is also evident in how the content matches the interests of children with the overall goals of the school. For example, lessons are made more interesting by the addition of easily understood legends, myths and historical events that model the cultural values being taught (truthfulness, compassion and tolerance). The principal explained the Ming Hui rationale behind using stories and provided some examples:

So you know their content, this is a complementary curriculum. Another one is, we also talk about Chinese culture, we emphasize on Chinese culture. Because Chinese culture is, you have study about it so you know that Chinese culture is very ancient, very profound, and a very rich content and substance. So we would have stories, the simplest one just like The Legend of Yue Fei, or Kong Rong Yields the Pears, or some stories that are easy for children to accept, to aid the children. After listening to the stories, they could understand the *zhōng xiào rén ài* in the stories [忠 *zhōng,* 孝 *xiào,* 仁 *rén,* 愛 *ài;* Confucian values of being loyal, filial, humane, and loving]. Why do you have to be filial to your parents? Why do we have to have these ancient Chinese customs? We use these stories to help deepen their impressions.

Aside from stories, the Ming Hui School has "music, dancing, martial arts, and drawing." What is aimed for in teaching these arts is *shényùn* (神韻 *shén* literally meaning *god, mysterious, soul or spirit* and *yùn* meaning *rhyme*), a term used in the arts to describe an esthetic value, expressing genuine feeling and sensitivity—not artificial or merely technically correct. In the following passage, the principal of the Ming Hui School explains how this concept is important in teaching the arts:

> Chinese dancing is about *shényùn*. *Shényùn* is what comes from within your heart, the manifestation of what you feel toward the dance, your like or dislike, and this is the outward expression...to let...the viewer...they can see what's contained inside...that it has meaning in it. It's not just some gestures...some random gestures...that is *shényùn.. shényùn....Shén* is the god or spirit above; *yùn* is the elegant or sophisticated style. So *shényùn* is like martial art, your spirits have to be there, and the display is from within your heart and mind, so you can touch the audience. So when we teach students the martial art or dancing or other subjects, we would teach about these matters too. It's not just about gesturing or moving of the fan here or there.

The choices made for language instruction are selected to maximize the cultural benefits while reducing the difficulty of mastering the language. For example, the traditional characters (ideograms) used in Taiwan and Hong Kong are taught instead of the simplified characters adopted by the PRC. The principal of the Ming Hui School explained the rationale as follows:

> But we still use the traditional character [正體 *zhèng tǐ*], that is the complicated character [繁體 *fán tǐ*], we don't teach the simplified character [簡體 *jiǎn tǐ*], I think you understand, simplified . . . they've changed so you don't know what meaning is inside, and Chinese character is, is truly, very rich content, and each character has its meaning contain in it. So if we use simplified, then the children won't know how we have the character, what is the origin? I think you have studied Chinese, so you know the meaning of a character evolved from pictograms [象形文 *xiàng xíng wén*]..... I think you know about it. This is because our children grew up here, so they were not exposed to these, these areas. So, that's why we put our emphasis on these areas.

From the preceding, it is clear that the principal believes that the simplified characters lack the depth of traditional characters, which contain clues to the meaning of the words, and which also maintain continuity with Chinese history. In short, traditional characters carry more culture and are not necessarily harder to learn.

The Ming Hui School uses the same student-centered approach in its choice of a phonetic system for teaching pronunciation of the Chinese characters. The Ming Hui School principal prefers to teach *hànyǔ pīnyīn* (漢語拼音), the phonetic system used in the PRC and Singapore, instead of *zhùyīn fúhào*

(注音符號), the phonetic system used in Taiwan. The principal explained the choice of transliteration method in the following way:

> And then when we teach Chinese, we use *hànyǔ pīnyīn*, or *zhùyīn fúhào*. But mostly *hànyǔ pīnyīn* is more emphasize because it is more readily accept by the children. . . . We still have *hànyǔ pīnyīn*, they are easy . . . easy to accept . . . it is adapt to their learning style.

This preference is rooted in convenience for the children, as *hànyǔ pīnyīn* uses the Roman alphabet with most sounds closely resembling English. *Zhùyīn fúhào*, however, is used only in Taiwan and has no resemblance to any other language, nor does it hold any ideographic key to the meaning of the Chinese characters.

It should be noted that the two methodological choices made for language instruction discussed above have no political overtones. In this case, there is no invective against communism for stripping out the roots of the Chinese ideograms, nor is the preference for the method used in Taiwan—so called "free China"—politically motivated. Rather, choices were made simply to make Chinese easier to learn, without losing anything linguistically significant, and all to maximize the language-learning experience. It should also be noted that though there are other phonetic systems used to transliterate Chinese, such as the Wade Giles system and the Yale system, these were neither used nor discussed. Perhaps the reason lies in the fact that these systems are falling into disuse as the PRC continues to rise in international influence.

Another salute to Chinese tradition in language instruction is the use of the *Three Character Classic* (三字經, *sān zì jīng*) and the *Thousand Word Essay* (千字文, *qiān zì wén*). The principal explains the method of vocabulary development thus: "As for our Chinese class, it's similar to a regular school where we start with lower level with recognizing the characters, but we would emphasize the *Three Character Classic* and *Thousand Word Essay*." These have been the basic primers for children since ancient times (the 13th century and the 6th century, respectively). Though they have fallen into relative disuse since the early 20th century, the Ming Hui School has restored them back to a place of honor as a basic literacy primer.

Aside from whatever language benefits may arise from these two texts, their cultural and moral impact must not be overlooked. The *Thousand Word Essay* is a beautiful piece of poetry, rooted in the ancient world. The oldest known Chinese language primer, the *Thousand Word Essay* uses exactly one thousand, non-redundant four-character rhyming couplets, with eight characters per line in seven chapters. Ultimately, the essay serves as a basic wordlist that touches on right conduct, the development of character, legendary figures and introduces the ancient cosmological worldview. The essay's poetic nature aids memory of the primary classical ideograms, which have been essential for success in traditional China and much of East Asia, including Korea, Japan and Vietnam, where Chinese has been the *lingua franca* and where the *Thousand Word Essay* has also gone. The historical importance of this text should be enough to bring it to the attention of anyone interested in Chinese culture, even children.

The *Three Character Classic* is also foundational, both for language and cultural development. Traditionally, parents would teach this text to their children, similar to the way in which present-day Americans teach the ABC's and nursery rhymes to their children. The *Three Character Classic*'s short lines of three characters prepare the child for mastery of the most common characters and grammatical structures, while also introducing the major people and events of Chinese history. And though it is not a Confucian classic, it embodies Confucian thought in a way young children can receive, as they have for centuries.

## Analysis of Ming Hui Content

The five exercises and the Zhuan Falun continue to maintain their central place in the lives of practitioners (in this case, children). These budding practitioners do the exercises and reflect on the truth contained in the Zhuan Falun, a text which will direct their thoughts in the construction of their worldview. This practice is believed to allow the mind and body to "change, ascend up"—in the words of the principal. Just as with adults, truthfulness, compassion and tolerance become the primary filter through which all knowledge, thought and activity are measured. According to the principal, "besides what I have just discussed, myth and legend of culture, virtues of loyalty and being filial [忠孝 zhōng xiào], we have the studying of fǎ [法, law] and practicing gōng [功, work]. I think this is what sets us apart from others."

The Ming Hui School uses an eclectic mix of traditional materials and modern methods to achieve its language and cultural learning objectives. Yet it should be pointed out that the principal originally stated that the goals of the school were the improvement of the students' temperament and the growth of the school itself. Based on all the interviews, the school's cultural learning goals coincide directly with the FLG vision of culture. Yet one might wonder whether the Chinese language is necessarily an objective in reaching these two goals. Of course, the Chinese language is intrinsically linked to Chinese culture. But it has already been noted that there are numerous translations available for adults to learn FLG. Why is Chinese language not pushed on American adults? It seems that the Ming Hui School focuses on Chinese immigrants who want their children to learn the Chinese language. This in itself does not seem to be a conflict, but it does seem to be an unstated strategic objective, supporting the school's primary goals.

## Restoration

The Ming Hui School provides what is perceived to have been lost—in the case of the children, the Chinese language and culture. One of the parents in the Ming Hui School confided that hers is the only child from a mixed marriage. There had been non-Chinese children in the past, but they moved to another state. All of the other children at the school were Chinese. This fact makes it clear that the Ming Hui School appeals primarily to Chinese practitioners, but not exclusively to them.

What is the attraction of the *Three Character Classic* and the *Thousand Word Essay*? Couldn't a more modern text be developed from a corpus of basic words? The answer lies, in part, with the fact that these primers are ancient, a characteristic especially compelling for a movement seeking to restore traditional culture. And, more importantly, the *Three Character Classic*, at least, teaches Confucian values—intrinsic to traditional Chinese culture and education and closely parallel to FLG values. The central FLG values of truthfulness, compassion and tolerance are not exactly parallel to the Confucian values of being loyal, filial, humane, and loving (忠 *zhōng*, 孝 *xiào*, 仁 *rén*, 愛, *ài*). Yet compassion assumes a humane and loving nature. Similarly, loyalty is a matter of being true to others, even at great cost to oneself. Indeed, the possibility of great cost, whether financial, or bodily suffering requires "tolerance" (in such a case best understood as endurance).

In short, the Ming Hui School's student-centered approach is to select ancient and modern materials and methods that facilitate skill-learning while, more importantly, promoting the FLG cultural values—truthfulness, compassion and tolerance. Finally, this culture is not legalistic or codified, but internalized.

## SUMMARY OF CHAPTER 4

In this chapter, I discussed how the ten in-depth interviews provided an understanding of how conversion and growth takes place in Falun Gong. A variety of socialization strategies attract new members and aid personal development through meditation in public parks, sharing and volunteerism, traditional and modern media, global digital networks, shows and demonstrations, digital guerilla activity, and weekend schools for children. Further, the central unifying theme for both content and methodology is seen as the principle of the universe—truthfulness, compassion and tolerance. In the next chapter, I will discuss how these same themes of socialization arise in the Falun Gong media.

*Chapter Five*

# Results: Socialization in FLG Media

The interviews in the previous chapter show how conversion and growth drive the process of socialization. This chapter investigates the themes that arise in various types of media. A survey of the various ways in which the messages of socialization are carried produces a vast array of FLG controlled technologies, from traditional media (such as letters, newspapers and posters) to advanced, digital technologies (such as e-mail, websites, hacking software, and satellite networks). Sometimes it is unclear how to classify the ways in which a message travels. A telephone call, for example, may be analogue or digital, carried over phone lines, radio waves (as in cell phones) or via satellites. And FLG shortwave radio is both broadcast traditionally and via satellite. Finally, media and content are sometimes inseparable, as in a stage drama that makes its way onto New Tang Dynasty Television and is later dispersed internationally in numerous print and digital formats.

The primary themes that arise in the interviews are also the primary themes in FLG media—Master Li, the nature of the universe as truthfulness, compassion and tolerance, karma, the five exercises for transforming the mind and body, healing, personal stories, sharing, volunteerism, the fight against communism, the ongoing persecution of FLG, restoration of traditional Chinese culture (including the arts), and teaching Chinese language and culture, and the good of society. Further, the importance of media in the participants' accounts suggests that they have all been shaped by similar media input.

## TRUTH, COMPASSION AND TOLERANCE

As in the interviews, the FLG media use truthfulness, compassion and tolerance as a gestalt, which appears in all of the media sampled: video disks, websites, blogs, radio, New Tang Dynasty Television, newspapers, posters and film. These cannot be separated, nor is one viewed as "higher" than another. In *Zhuan Falun*, Master Li says that both Daoist and Buddhist schools cultivate truthfulness, compassion (benevolence, good) and tolerance (endurance, forbearance). They are "what Daoists call 'the Dao,' or what Buddhists call 'the Law'" (H. Li, 2003, p. 1). But the two schools are different in that Daoists focus on cultivating the true and Buddhists focus on cultivating compassion. FLG is best because it balances the principles of the universe.

> Our Falun Dafa discipline, the Law Wheel Great Way, goes by the highest standard of the universe, to be True, Good, and Endure, and we cultivate these all together. So what we cultivate is huge. (H. Li, 2003, p. 8)

In FLG, truth (真, zhēn) is rooted in the nature of the universe—truthfulness, compassion and tolerance. The problem is that few people know the truth, and that Li is "the only person in the world who is publicly spreading a true teaching" (H. Li, 2003, p. 51). Truth is found in becoming like the universe. Truth is in returning to one's true nature, one's true self which was lost ages ago by taking on attachments. Truth is obtained through reducing one's own karma and in teaching others to do the same:

> When a person wants to return back up from this dimension, to do what Daoist practices call "returning to the original, true self," he will need to put his heart into cultivation, which means his Buddha-nature has come out. And that wish is considered the most precious one. So people will help him. Even in such a tough environment, he hasn't gotten lost and still wants to return, so people will help him, they'll help him unconditionally, and they'll help him with anything. And why can we do that for cultivators but not for ordinary people? That's why. (H. Li, 2003, p. 35)

In FLG, the word *clarification* is closely associated with truth. Truth, of course, is a noun, but clarification is what the practitioner does with it. Clarifying the truth is an action most often understood in FLG circles as finding ways to combat persecution. Indeed, one FLG website glossary defines clarifying the truth as helping "people understand Falun Gong, to dispel the lies of the communist regime in China against Falun Gong, and to raise public support to end the persecution" (Glossary, n.d., para. 3). Master Li, however, seems to view this focus as problematic and needing correction. He recently posted a note telling practitioners that clarifying the truth is about saving people, not about human rights work:

> The Human Rights Torch Relay does involve working against persecution and helping people to see the evil party for what it is, but it cannot take the place of

clarifying the truth to save people. The Human Rights Torch Relay has everyday people as its driving force and was initiated for the purpose of exposing and resisting the evil party's persecution of the Chinese people, so it is not to be passed to Dafa disciples. Dafa disciples in Mainland China should not set aside their truth-clarification work and participate on a large scale. (H. Li, 2008, para. 1)

In short, clarifying the truth is practicing and sharing FLG, not doing good works. This redefinition of what one does with truth should also be seen as a rejection of the view that FLG is a political movement.

A synonym of clarification is rectification. The practitioner must rectify the *Fa*. One practitioner quotes Master Li as saying, "We rectify all that which has deviated from Dafa" (A. Feng, May 14, 2001, para. 1). The practitioner, whose article has been on a major FLG website since May 2001, explains how this is applied:

It is almost unimaginable that our body can be changed/purified in the course of our individual cultivation. The key is to transform one's thoughts first. The same rule applies to the integrated cultivation of all of us. We all need to transform our thoughts first; then we can make the breakthrough that will change our condition. (para. 4)

In other words, Fa-rectification begins with cultivation of the mind. As cultivation continues, the body also becomes purified, changed, as the whole person rises to higher levels. In doing the fifth exercise, a meditation, this is an altered state, but it must also be a metacognitive process. This becomes clear as the writer continues:

Some are still blissfully going deep into trance and losing awareness, not really cultivating his/her own main spirit. . . . To do Fa-rectification in [a mutated environment] we must bind closely with the Dafa at every moment. This is the only way we won't drift. The Fa-rectifying process is our cultivating process; Fa is in the process of nurturing and establishing us as well (para. 12).

## Compassion

Compassion seems to be subsumed under truth, not exactly on par with it, because both the interviews and the FLG media tend to cite compassion as a value or motivation behind telling the truth—promoting FLG. Telling the truth is compassionate in that FLG ultimately cures all ills, whether one's own sickness or one's own karma or the problems of society. When compassion is mentioned, it is in direct connection to truth-telling, not in doing good deeds for their own sake. Giving, for example, is not to the poor, but to FLG activities. Similarly, though healing is possible, Master Li forbids it. In fact, the act of healing another person requires a transfer of merit from one's own *gong*, and is therefore seen as harmful to the healer's health and moral character. In the *Zhuan Falun*, Master Li explains his rational:

> No true cultivator of Falun Dafa may heal people. As soon as you do healing, my Law Bodies will take back all the Falun Dafa things that your body carries. Why do we take this so seriously? Because it's something that damages Dafa. Not only does it harm your own health, but some people just itch to do it again once they've healed something, and they'll grab whoever they see to treat them and show off. Isn't that an attachment? It will have a serious impact on your cultivation. (H. Li, 2003, p. 144)

The prohibition on healing is not to say that healing is not important; it is. But poor health is a symptom of karma. The root problem must be addressed. This is done through introducing FLG. Master Li recommends "reading this book to a sick person, and if he can accept its contents, it can heal him, but how effective it is depends on how much karma he has" (p. 147). Thus, each person should heal themselves through practicing FLG. In short, as FLG is the cure, sharing this truth, is the most compassionate thing someone can do.

## Tolerance

Though practitioners hold on to their beliefs and practices even when threatened with torture or harm to family and friends, the value of tolerance must not be equated with a death wish or even sadomasochism. There is no evidence for a love of suffering. Rather, it is an appreciation for its value. Through suffering one may transform karma into virtue and ultimately improve one's level. Furthermore, enduring suffering may further advance truth and compassion for others. When others see how practitioners are able to take suffering with equanimity, they may be impressed enough to accept FLG themselves. Hence, the process is both truth-telling and compassionate.

## THE INTERNET

Discussing FLG's use of the media in socialization without mentioning the Internet is virtually impossible. Virtually every method and strategy employed is enhanced through the Internet. Though traditional media, such as books and newspapers, continue to be produced and sold in traditional ways, the Internet provides ways of multiplying the reach and reducing the overall cost of these media. For example, anyone desiring a hardcopy of *Zhuan Falun* or *The Epoch Times* newspaper can obtain one from a traditional bookstore or through a FLG website (such as www.tiantibooks.com) or from a non-FLG website (such as www.amazon.com). Furthermore, anyone who does not have access to a traditional bookstore selling FLG books or who cannot afford to buy them can simply download them for free from a FLG website, such as (www.falundafa. org/eng/books.html), or from a non-FLG website (such as www.memoware. com). Those who have been blocked from downloading FLG materials can use firewall-busting software, also produced by FLG practitioners.

There are many types of FLG websites. Most sites have a sophisticated but clear design with a large collection of material for download in a variety of formats, including text, photos, audio and video, but all are dedicated to socializing others into a FLG worldview based on truthfulness, compassion and tolerance. Just as a worldview must address a broad variety of human concerns, so do FLG websites, from introductory sites (www.falundafa.org) that provide contact information for local practice sites and free downloads of Master Li's teachings, to specific genres, such as art (www.falunart. org), news (www.epochtimes.com), politics (www.chinaaffairs.org), FLG schools (www.minghui-school.org), dance (http://divineperformingarts.org), film (www.sandstormmovie.com), television (www.fgmtv.org; www.ntdtv. com; http://cntv.us), radio (http://soundofhope.org; www.falundafaradio.org ; www.mhradio.org), and human rights (www.flghrwg.net). Some are even family sites, dedicated to getting a father home (http://freezhiwen.org).

Finally, besides content sites, there are enabling sites that make the transfer of content possible when national firewalls attempt to censor FLG material. For example, Dynamic Internet Technology (http://www.dit-inc.us) provides a proxy network, DynaWeb, for circumventing Internet censorship in China. When a user in China runs the provided encryption software, they contact DynaWeb, which decrypts the signals, collects the desired data and sends it back encrypted. Meanwhile, China's Internet police are unable to detect the nature of the sites visited. All of this happens seamlessly, so the user is able to browse the web, just as if there were no firewall.


## FIVE EXERCISES

### Learning the Exercises from the Books

The five exercises are an important theme in most FLG media. *Falun Gong* (H. Li, 2001), the book, whether the hardcopy or a downloaded version, describes how to do the five exercises, step-by-step in great detail, explaining what to do and why, as well as what not to do. *Falun Gong* also shows photos of Master Li doing the exercises. The assumption seems to be that there is no better model than the Master himself. *Zhuan Falun* (H. Li, 2003) also talks extensively about the exercises, but its focus is cultivation in the larger sense, explaining how the exercises fit into the overall worldview.


## Learning the Exercises from the Internet

Aside from the foundational books, several FLG web sites aid learning by providing multimedia downloads of Master Li teaching the exercises (Exercise Music, n.d.; Exercises, n.d.; Free Downloads, 2002).

Many sites, however, also show practitioners of various ethnicities doing the exercises, not just Master Li (www.falundafa.gr; www.pureinsight. org; www.falundafa.ie/main/main.htm; www.faluninfo.net). These materials, however, are not so much for teaching the exercises, but rather for sharing and growth. Though it is not directly stated, is seems that the purpose of highlighting the racial variety is to show that FLG is for everyone, regardless of cultural background or race. Anyone visiting across such sites might be more likely to be drawn to the movement.


## Learning the Exercises at the Parks

As indicated in the interviews, the FLG media provide evidence that performing the exercises in the parks promotes conversion, both in reality and by design. It is, indeed, easy to find practitioners who were initially attracted to FLG through viewing the exercises. The FLG media provides overwhelming examples, such as the practitioner who describes what happened in 1998 in North Carolina when he saw a young man doing FLG meditation: "Something stronger than my own wish was pushing me to talk with him . . . on the third day I couldn't hold my strong desire to talk with that gentleman . . . .my life has changed" (Andrade, 1999, para. 4). A practitioner from the Ming Hui School in Taiwan describes how one woman was drawn to FLG after seeing the children practicing their morning exercises in a park near the school: "when the woman saw all the young practitioners practising [sic] Falun Gong, she suddenly became interested and decided to learn it right on the spot" (Taiwan Minghui, 2004, para. 6).

As one practitioner interviewed in this study pointed out, practicing in the park does not resonate with Buddhist practices, where meditation should be done in seclusion in order to reduce distractions. It does, however, fit with Daoism, where conforming with the Dao is best done in a natural setting. Indeed, many have noted how China's elderly have had the practice of rising early to practice Taichi (太極, tàijí) in the parks (Lam, 2004; Moyers, 1995).

Aside from China's historical-cultural affinity with practicing morning exercises in public, FLG's insistence on practicing in the parks is clearly designed to attract people. This is seen in two recent official statements. When mainland practitioners contact Minghui Radio about whether or not it is acceptable for them to use MP3 recordings of the exercise music instead of the live broadcast, Minghui responds that it is fine, but they add, "It is suggested that those practitioners who are outside of China and those Mainland practitioners in suitable situations go outside to do the exercises, while those practitioners in areas of Mainland China where the conditions are not ripe should avoid going to extremes" (About the early, 2008, para. 4). In other words, because of the danger of severe persecution, there is no need to practice in public. This would be "extreme." There is no hint that practice indoors might be less efficacious. Those in "suitable conditions," read *safe*, are not given such a dispensation. They should practice outside. Practicing in the parks is not only for the self but to socialize others.

How the exercises are used as socialization comes sharply into focus in an article by a Singapore practitioner who traveled with a group of seventeen others to promote FLG in Vietnam. Their method was twofold: "practice the exercises and distribute materials" (My experience, 2008, para. 1). This phrase is repeated almost verbatim two more times. Indeed, the word *exercise* appears eight times and the word *materials* appears eleven times. During the trip, the practitioners taught both locals as well as "black and Caucasian people who came to learn" (para. 4).

### Nine-Day Seminars

Though any practice site will provide "on-the-spot" (Falun Dafa, 2008b, para. 1) instruction in the exercises for free, the most "comprehensive" (Learning, 2008, para. 6) way to learn the exercises is in a Nine Day Seminar, which consists of watching videos of nine lectures given by Master Li between 1992 and 1994. During the seminars, local practitioners answer questions and teach the exercises. The topics covered in the seminars include the following: truthfulness, compassion and tolerance; distinctions between *qigong* and Falun Dafa; why *qigong* heals; how *qigong* differs from physical exercise; how to increase energy with practice; and why one should cultivate to return to one's original self (Falun Dafa, 2008a). Seminars are arranged upon request and provided for free, gifts not accepted. Of course, the audio and video files of the original seminars are available as a free download (9-Day, 2007; Audio, 2007).

## VOLUNTEERISM

It is the policy in FLG to teach the exercises for free. The learners do not pay, nor are the teachers reimbursed. In the FLG journal *Compassion*, one practitioner expresses this succinctly: "All practice sites teach the exercises free of charge and are organized by volunteers" (Parker, 2004, p. 41). This policy is based not simply on a whim or even an educational theory but on the intrinsic value of the message and the value of the learner. Indeed, in *Zhuan Falun*, the Master says:

> We give you so many things, and you couldn't put a price on them. Why do we give them to you? For you to cultivate! We can only give you all this when you cultivate. Then what this means is that down the road when you pass on the practice to other people, you can't use these things to go make a name for yourself or benefit yourself. (H. Li, 2003, p. 69)

The seriousness of Li's injunction comes across as he lays down a rule and the consequence of breaking the rule:

> The first rule is that you can't charge any money. We don't give you all those things so that you can get rich and famous, but to save you, to help you cultivate. If you charge money my Law Bodies will take everything back from you, and you won't belong to our Falun Dafa, so what you spread won't be our Falun Dafa. When you pass on the practice you shouldn't have any thoughts about making a name for yourself, or getting something out of it—you should help them voluntarily. Our students all across the country have been doing it that way, and the Assistants in different regions have set an example. Anybody who wants to learn our practice, you can come and learn it, you just have to want to, and we can take responsibility for you and we won't charge you a cent (H. Li, 2003, p. 69).

Volunteerism is rooted in compassion and tolerance—compassionate in that sharing the truth is aiding others, and tolerant in that it costs the teacher to teach. It takes the teacher's time; and sometimes, the teacher even provides the learner with materials for study. Indeed, during the course of this research, FLG practitioners gave of their time and provided free materials and food, nor would they accept any remuneration. Volunteerism is so rooted in the nature of FLG that seeking remuneration would cause the Law Bodies—emanations from Master Li which are sent to protect the practitioner—to leave.

From an educational and institutional standpoint, volunteerism may aid in conversion in that it dispenses with questions of financial gain as the motivation behind local practitioner's sharing. Instead of hard-sell tactics (except on human rights issues), the learner is faced with the non-pushy approach of sharing. The prospective learner has nothing to lose, except the time it takes to try out the exercises.

For the movement in general, volunteerism provides free labor. For individuals, volunteerism is a reward in itself. Indeed, volunteers should refuse payment in order to maintain the benefits of their good works, which the practitioner's falun turns into virtue.

From a tactical standpoint, volunteerism promotes creative thinking and participation. As there are no clergy, everyone has responsibility to himself, and, of course, to Master Li, to apply whatever talents, ideas and energies he may have to advancing the movement, thereby bringing salvation to himself and others. Whether the skills are writing programs to circumvent firewalls, translating Master Li's writings, posting articles on FLG websites or working for FLG television, the technical knowledge base and creativity of the practitioners propel FLG's many approaches to sharing the *Fa* with the world.

## INDIVIDUAL AND GROUP SHARING

Individual sharing and group sharing are similar in that in both cases, individuals tell their stories: how they came to FLG and what life has been like since. As seen in the interviews, when asked, "Tell me how you became involved with Falun Gong;" and "tell me what it has been like to be involved with Falun Gong," they did not reply with desiccated points or causes and effects. Rather, they replied with their life stories. Similarly, in the FLG media, sharing centers on the stories of individuals. What their lives were like before FLG, and how they have changed for the better in terms of health and character of mind. Of course, a large percentage of stories (especially from China) tells of persecution, which is not enjoyable but is seen as an opportunity for greater karma reduction.

Aside from stories being told one to one and in local practice groups, practitioners regularly gather for large experience-sharing conferences. For example, at the Minneapolis conference in 2007, practitioners from 15 states gathered to hear 19 speakers tell their stories (Jing, 2007). And at the Los Angeles conference in 2008, "about 20 Falun Gong practitioners shared their cultivation experiences with 1,500 practitioners in the audience" (Huang & Ying, 2008, para. 1).

## DEMONSTRATIONS, PARADES AND SHOWS

FLG practitioners put on demonstrations, participate in parades, and put on shows in order to share their message of salvation or of the need for justice. The demonstrations take place around government sites in order to attract the attention of those governments and anyone passing by. For example, outside the Chinese embassies and consulates, FLG practitioners are regularly seen picketing, heard shouting slogans (Protesters, 2008; United States, 2008) and holding candlelight vigils (Los Angeles, 2008)—causing the diplomatic staff to look for ways to suppress FLG even in the United States (Dillow, 2008; Morais, 2006; Rosett, 2002).

## Parades

Ostensibly, participation in parades is a way to celebrate cultural festivals. FLG practitioners participate with their standard themes: traditional Chinese culture, FLG exercises and persecution in China. For example, in the 2008 Thanksgiving Parade in Chicago, the FLG contingent contributed the traditional dragon dance (including non-Chinese individuals), some fairies, a float of practitioners doing FLG exercises (some sitting inside giant lotuses), and flag carriers (NTDTV, 2008). And in the *Karneval der Kulturen* in Hamburg Germany, the FLG debuted a marching band at a cultural festival (Germany, 2007).

As a result of parade activities, FLG has become more widely known, not simply because of the parade participation but because of controversy surrounding the participation. Beijing has used every political and economic tactic available in order to block FLG participation in the San Francisco Chinese New Year parade since 2006 (Hua, 2006; Marshall, 2006), and in the San Gabriel Chinese New Year parade, though failing to block them from the San Francisco Bay Area annual St Patrick's Day parade (Wang, 2008) or Chinese New Year parades in New York (Caiju & Huang, 2007) and Chicago (NTDTV, 2008), or the Hollywood Christmas parade (Practitioners Bring, 2007) or from starting their own parade in Los Angeles (Falun Gong Holds, 2008).

## Shows

Perhaps the most elaborate and attractive presentation of the FLG worldview is the Chinese New Year Spectacular, which began in New York five years ago and has been adding cities to the tour ever since, is expected to perform in over 60 cities around the world with a total attendance of 650,000 (J. Li, 2007). Produced by New Tang Dynasty Television, the spectacular includes:

> dances inspired by ancient Chinese mythology and Chinese ethnic folk dances. The show also features classical Chinese vocal performances, instrumental music and classical Chinese dance. The Divine Performing Arts Troupe intends to deliver a pure, sincere and kind world. The combination of the beautifully designed scenes, music, and dance will deliver the essence of traditional Chinese divine culture. (J. Li, 2007, para. 7)

From the quotation above, it is clear how the show relates to traditional culture. What should not be overlooked is the phrase "divine culture" and the delivering of a "kind world." What is intended is not just a show, but a show that delivers a different type of world to the audience—a "pure, sincere and kind world," a divine world. The show does not directly proselytize. However, once the new worldview has been delivered, the expectation seems to be that the audience will treasure it, perhaps even turning to the practice of FLG.

There seem to be only two types of reaction to the spectacular: love or hate. Those who love the spectacular are not few in number. The FLG media has no shortage of positive reactions to the show, of course, made by non-practitioners, both in text (Belgium, 2008; Little, 2008) and audio-visual (Brisbane, 2008). Furthermore, even secular media have positive reviews providing accurate description and quotations from interviews with the cast. For example, the *Boston Globe* describes the Chinese New Year Spectacular as having dozens of performers, who "sweep across the stage in richly colored costumes, telling stories through movement and music" (Byrne, 2008, p. D5); it is "Andrew Lloyd Webber meets Chinese Folk Tales" (Fahey, 2007, p. Reg7). If the show were not appreciated, how could it have been rated "the seventh-largest show in attendance in the United States" in 2006 (p. Reg7). And how could it afford to play "on some of the world's finest stages from New York to London" (When art, 2008, April 12)?

There are few media detractors, but they do exist. One reviewer for *The Star* had little good to say about the show, calling it "spectacularly tacky" (Walker, 2008 , para. 2), "banal" (para. 5), "under-rehearsed and unremarkable" (para. 5). Whether or not the technical criticism is valid, clearly the primary problem is that the writer wanted entertainment, not FLG propaganda:

Truth that was offered up at every opportunity in a presentation of "the true essence of Chinese culture" before it was "damaged by the Chinese Communist Party." The production is so heavily laden with Falun Gong messages as to negate any pleasure the dancing and singing might have afforded. (Walker, 2008 , para. 2)

The other major detractor, of course, is the Chinese government which looks for every opportunity to thwart the Chinese New Year Spectacular, from putting pressure on sponsors (Haithman, 2008) to putting pressure on foreign governments—effective pressure on South Korea (Fahey, 2007) and Malaysia (Malaysia, 2008), but less so with Australia (When art, 2008, April 12) and the United States of America (Berthelsen, 2008; Dillow, 2008; Haithman, 2008).

## BANKNOTES

Besides the financial cost of creating and disseminating FLG media—certainly astronomical, but not a theme in either the interviews or the FLG publications—the use of money is one of the most novel and low-tech approaches to sharing the *Fa*. The method is simple. Practitioners write messages on money. As the banknotes circulate through society, so do the FLG messages. One practitioner describes her approach:

> I read a fellow practitioners' sharing on the Internet that they have begun to clarify the truth by writing messages on money. I did the same and began using bills to clarify the truth. Every day I had to buy things like groceries and other materials. Before going out I would first write on all the bills that were 10 Yuan and under. Then, I would send forth righteous thoughts before going out. Every day I would spend a dozen or so bills. Sometimes when I finished using these bills, I wouldn't want to use the bills that were not written on. (Cultivating well, 2008, para. 6)

This practice, of course, is not without repercussions. Two days earlier, the Clearwisdom site records that a doctor in Daqing was arrested for using "bills with truth clarification messages printed on them" (Additional persecution, 2008, para. 8); another doctor at a private clinic, also "involved in the case" was arrested the next day and detained for two weeks. The same page names three others, including two middle-school teachers, who were arrested for the same practice.

## PRINT AND SHARING

Aside from the books *Falun Gong* (H. Li, 2001) and *Zhuan Falun,* (H. Li, 2003), which are always the primary texts for socialization, FLG has a number of other print media aiding both sharing and growth. For example, Master Li has written a follow-up text to *Zhuan Falun—Falun Dafa: Essentials for Further Advancement* (H. Li, 2000), a collection of short writings meant to help practitioners better understand *Zhuan Falun*.

FLG practitioners also produce a number of books usually about how FLG changed their lives. For example, *Witnessing History* (Zeng, 2006), a 368-page book, is the story of how one woman in China found FLG, was persecuted and finally escaped to the West. Shorter personal stories also appear in anthologies (Culp, 1999; Personal, 2008).

Another practitioner publication is *Compassion Journal*, which presents articles largely focused on the persecution of FLG in China. This journal, however, has an irregular publishing schedule. This is probably due to the fact that it is run totally by volunteers.

A FLG publication with a broader appeal is *The Epoch Times* weekly newspaper, which provides hard news, especially news of the persecution, as well as regional and local news.

In August 2000, a group of FLG practitioners launched *The Epoch Times* newspaper both in print and on the Internet in New York. Since then, the paper has grown phenomenally and now claims to be the most widely distributed paper in the world, available in 29 countries and with regional offices in the United States (12 total, 2 in Southern California), the UK, Canada, Australia, Ireland, New Zealand, Germany, Taiwan, Hong Kong, Japan and Indonesia. Aside from its general availability, *The Epoch Times* is printed in 10 languages and 17 on the Internet. In New York, the print edition has been printed daily since June 12, 2008. Elsewhere, it comes out every Thursday, with the Internet edition updated daily and with breaking news.

*The Epoch Times* is available for free at many local Chinese bookstores and supermarkets in the Los Angeles area, as in many other cities. However, a subscription is available for $78. Publishing costs of the newspaper are primarily defrayed by the sale of advertizing space.

*The Epoch Times* maintains an extensive Internet site, also free, with national editions focusing on the United States, Canada, Australia, the United Kingdom, Ireland, and New Zealand—as well as an internationally focused edition. Anyone wishing to read *The Epoch Times* may download daily articles from the website. If readers wish to read past print issues, they, too, are available for a free download (even localized editions for Boston, Dallas, Los Angeles, New York, San Francisco, Southeast U.S., Washington D.C., as well as Australia, Ireland, Malaysia, New Zealand, Singapore and the UK, and four cities in Canada) in Adobe's portable document file (pdf)—original artwork and advertisements included.

*The Epoch Times* articles cover everything that other major online newspapers cover. In fact, many of the articles come from Reuters. Of course, a large percentage of the articles deal with events of particular concern to the FLG—such as human rights issues in China and around the world, as well as FLG run events, such as the Chinese New Year Spectacular.

*The Epoch Times* also posts a count of the number of people denouncing and resigning from the Chinese Communist Party. Next to the number-count is a link to *The Nine Commentaries on the Communist Party*. These commentaries, a special publication of *The Epoch Times*, tell the story of how the Communist Party, since it took power, has destroyed Chinese culture and tortured and murdered its citizens.

## TELEPHONES

## Cold Calling China

One FLG website (http://www.clarifythetruthinchina.com) provides scripts and accompanying audio files for explaining the truth of the persecution to individuals in China by phone and fax. In a private correspondence, an *Epoch Times* editor explained the reason for this: "Many Chinese do not believe the persecution against FLG is true and that FLG practitioners are not good people because of the state-run media and government propaganda." In short, practitioners call China and read the scripts, play the audio files or send the fax to whoever answers the phone. In order to fit the needs of the practitioner, various approaches are provided.

Of course, there are scripts in Chinese for readers of Chinese. Yet to meet the need of non-Chinese readers who will be contacting Chinese speakers (who are unlikely to understand English), audio files are available for download with scripts in Chinese (including phonetic transliteration) as well as English translation of the scripts. To top it off, there is a step-by-step explanation of suggested ways to use the materials.

For example, after someone in China picks up the phone, "we say to them in our best 'Western-Chinese': '*Ni Hao!* . . . *Fa lun Da fa Hao* . . . Fa lun Da fa Hao' which means, of course, "Hello! Falun Dafa is Good . . . Falun Dafa is Good'" (How to make, n.d., para. 1). Aside from help with the pronunciation, western practitioners are reminded of what to think, feel and visualize:

> However, when we say the words "Fa lun Da fa Hao", we always say them slowly, very calmly, and with the deepest heart-felt sincerity -- almost like what we're saying is coming from our heart and not from our mouths. We clearly feel the person on the other end of the phone being effected [sic] by the calm, righteous, and genuine solemness [sic] of our words.

> Then we play the "Irina Phone Script" for them . . .

> While the voice-recording is playing, we picture an innocent being who has been deceived into thinking that Falun Gong is bad and we clear out the interference surrounding that person's dimensional field.

Various types of recordings are provided to go with the scripts, such as male and female voices, as wells as those of an eleven year old boy and an eight year old girl. The shorter scripts ask the listener not to persecute FLG because it is good. Note how these include the phonetic Chinese pronunciation.

Hello.
*Ni3 Hao3*
I am an American person.
*Wo3 shi4 mei3 guo2 ren2*
Falun Dafa is a righteous way.
*Fa3 Lun2 Da4 Fa3 Shi4 Zheng4 Fa3*
Stop persecuting Zhen Shan Ren.
*Ting2 zhi3 po4 hai4 Zhen1 Shan4 Ren3*
Falun Dafa is Good.
*Fa3 lun2 Da4 fa3 Hao3*
The whole world knows Falun Dafa is good.
*Quan2 shi4 jie4 zhi1 dao4 Fa3 lun2 da4 fa3 Hao3*
Thank you.
*Xie4 xie4* (Learn simple, n.d., para. 4)

Longer scripts add how the government is persecuting FLG:

This is a 3 minutes [sic] "truth-news" announcement. Since July 1999. Jiang
Zemin ordered the crackdown on Falun Gong (FLG). Thousands of FLG
families in China have been destroyed. FLG practitioners have been subject
to forced brainwashing. If they don't give in, they will be fined large sums of
money, detained illegally, put into labor camps or jail; beaten, injected with
poison, and even tortured to death. Numerous tragedies have occurred. On
April 20, 2000, a US Wall-street newspaper reported from Shandong Province,
that Chen Zixiu, 58, was tortured to death because she did not want to give up
FLG. The witness in this case said the persecution was very crazy. She died on
Feb. 21, 2000. A teacher in Beijing Industry and Business college, Zhao Xin,
32, was tortured to death just because she went to Zizhuyuan to practice the
FLG exercises. She died on Dec.11, 2000. Till today, there are 468 FLG practitioners that have been secretly tortured to death in 30 provinces. The Chinese
government has tortured more than 1600 FLG practitioners. There are more
than 600 FLG practitioners who were illegally sentenced to jail. Thousands of
FLG practitioners were put into mental institutions. They were injected with
medicine that destroyed their nervous system. More than 100,000 FLG practitioners have been illegally put into labor camps. Numerous FLG practitioners
have been subject to brainwashing courses. More people were beaten and
fined by the police. (Script 04, n.d., para. 1)

If someone wants to share the news of FLG with China, they need numbers. This problem has already been solved. In the left column of the website
(www.clarifythetruthinchina.com), there are three useful links taking the visitor to pages designed to provide three types of numbers: business, media, and
prison / police. The business numbers are not simply displayed; the visitor
has to e-mail the website (Business phone, n.d.). Perhaps this is to make sure

that businesses are contacted in a more random fashion in order to prevent feelings of harassment.

The media numbers require some work to obtain as well. Clicking on the link provided takes the visitor to either a Yahoo directory (News and media, 2008) or a China site directory (Complete reference, 2008). This might be because Yahoo and Chinasite will keep these numbers updated. Such a strategy will save the FLG sites time and effort in overall maintenance.

A much more difficult set of numbers to obtain and maintain are those that are not published, especially the numbers of those involved in the persecution of FLG practitioners. Overseas practitioners, however, have somehow obtained an amazing list of phone numbers (home, mobile and office) of mayors, Public Security Bureau officers, labor camps directors, and detention camps. Even the home phone numbers of some party secretaries are included (Prison officials, n.d.). The same page reminds the visitor, "Teacher has said, 'Every phone call from our students shocks them [the police, prison guards, and prison officials] to the point that they can't sleep at night.' I expect this to be true, if only because of the difference in time zones—12 noon in California is 3 a.m. in China.

## Funding the Cold Calling

When FLG practitioners call China, the expense comes out of their own pockets. Nevertheless, *The Epoch Times* is makes calling China cheaper by selling competitively priced phone cards, at the time of this writing, 1.5 cents per minute (http://phonecard.dajiyuan.com). Aside from sales to FLG members, the card may find customers through Internet searches and banners. Afterward, the sale is likely to promote FLG, because the card carries the logo of *The Epoch Times* newspaper.

## Texting and Online Chatting

As cell phones are becoming popular communication devices worldwide, so is texting, which is sending a text message to another mobile phone or computer. This fact has not been lost on FLG practitioners who send short messages, or even the entire *Nine Commentaries*. One practitioner in Beijing noted, "there are currently 500 million cell phone users in mainland China. Text messaging will have an enormous impact" (C. Feng, 2008, para. 9). That is about half of the population. Embracing this technology has become a primary strategy for promoting growth of FLG and attacking the Chinese Communist Party. A Taiwan practitioner whose pastime entails helping mainlanders quit the Chinese Communist Party explained the strategy: "Telephone, mobile phone text messages, chatting online are the main channels we use to deliver our message"(Wen, 2007, para. 2).

An even more savvy approach is the multimedia text message. A user in Wuxi, China told *The Epoch Times* that he received an animated FLG message with Christmas songs and three options: "Please press 1 to quit CCP, press 2 to quit CCP's Youth League (CYL), press 3 to quit CCP's Young Pioneer League (CYP)" (C. Feng, 2008, para. 4). Thus, not only sending messages from friend to friend is easier, but quitting the Chinese Communist Party is easier. The user also told the Epoch Times that he sent the message to his friends "because of the Christmas song," (para. 5), who replied, "smart, that's really clever."

## E-Mail

A Christian student from China told me that in China she often received unsolicited e-mails claiming that FLG is good and should not be persecuted by the government. Indeed, evidence of such practices does exist. For example, Dynamic Internet Technology (DIT) provides Internet service for users in countries with strong Internet censorship (www.dit-inc.us). DIT's clients include the United States government, *The Epoch Times*, Voice of America (VOA), Radio Free Asia (RFA), and Human Rights in China (HRIC). DIT stays abreast of e-mail blocking technologies in order to circumvent such censorship. Aside from sending "billions of emails to China for VOA and RFA" (Mass mailing, 2002, para. 1), DIT has also "delivered the Chinese version of *Nine Commentaries* to 2.3 million email addresses in China" (para. 3) for *The Epoch Times*.

## MARKETING

As I was reviewing themes on *The Epoch Times* website, a popup window appeared asking if the visitor was willing to take a marketing survey. I was. From the beginning, the survey made it clear that the respondent would be entered into a drawing for a 26 inch LCD television. The survey asked about personal data (such as name, e-mail address, home address, income, purchasing responsibilities within the family, and education level) impression of the site for reliable quality, and media preferences (such as paper, TV, radio). It also asked whether the visitor was aware of Epoch Times' media partners (NTDTV and Sound of Hope Radio). The survey concluded with thanking the visitor for answering the survey and of the possibility of winning the television.

This marketing strategy, of course, is a common tactic for Internet businesses because it provides fast and easily manipulated data at a relatively low cost of collection. But the tactic is notable because FLG usually gives away information or instruction on FLG culture. It is an example of how FLG is willing to adopt common cultural practices in order to more effectively carry out its mission. In this case, the mission is providing local and world news from a FLG perspective.


## DIGITAL GUERILLA ACTIVITY

I invented the term digital guerilla activity to label the category made up of various digital activities of FLG which aid conversion and growth by providing a number of networking options (e.g., firewall circumventing software and related servers; news, education and spiritual help websites; forums for protest against the Chinese government; and attack on Chinese government telecommunications infrastructure).


### Circumventing Firewalls

During the course of data collection, I attempted to access a FLG webpage in Chinese. Unfortunately, the university where I was doing this research blocked the page for suspected racism and hate speech. Having seen the English translation of the page, I knew there was no racism or hate on the page. So I assumed that the university's censoring software was oversensitive. At this point, I decided it was time to try out one of the FLG tools for circumventing firewalls. These tools are software programs that encrypt data to and from FLG servers which connect the surfer to the uncensored Internet.

There are five popular anticensorship tools developed by the Global Internet Freedom Consortium: FirePhoenix, GPass, GTunnel, FreeGate and UltraSurf. I downloaded all five programs from the consortium's website (www. internetfreedom.org) and attempted to install. My antivirus software warned that FirePhoenix and GTunnel were infected with Trojan horses, so the installation of these two was cancelled. It is probable that they were not infected but were merely identified as such because of their tunneling capabilities. The other three, FreeGate, GPass and UltraSurf, installed without any warnings.

Then I tried out each of the installed programs to see whether the university firewall would still be a problem. Immediately, the desired webpage was viewable, with no perceived lag time in transfer rates, even though the programs encrypted all data coming and going over the lines.

At this point, I wondered whether the FLG had its own form of censorship. Remembering that sexual immorality was anathema to FLG because it increases karma (Law of cause, 2005; Rooting out, 2008; Zheng, 2006), I decided to attempt to access pornographic material. In order to make sure that the results were based on the FLG software and servers and not the local firewall, I did this second round of testing from a location known to be without a firewall. Pornography was blocked. Yet all other types of data were easily downloadable —news, blogs, audio, video—regardless of origin. These two tests reveal how FLG provides solutions to perceived digital tyranny, while maintaining commitment to traditional moral values.

## Digital Invasion

FLG members have been known to take temporary control of government digital infrastructure—such as cable television (Whoever plays, 2002) and satellite broadcasting (Tanner, 2002)—to broadcast FLG themes. Of course, the government sees this as an attack on property and sovereignty. However, the FLG sees such strategies as a way to tell the truth: that the Chinese government should stop human rights abuses and that FLG is good. Though such tactics show the sophistication of FLG's digital prowess, and though perhaps the common people are impressed with the unexpected message from FLG, such digital attacks do not necessarily bring about the intended results. For the government both updates their technology to avoid interference (China plans, 2004) and also becomes more resolute to stamp out FLG. Indeed, it seems FLG has not continued to pursue this type of digital attack.

## Declarations

Another weapon is an ongoing count of individuals who sign a declaration renouncing or denouncing the Chinese Communist Party. The count on all versions of *the Epoch Times* is over 47 million at the time of this writing. On the main page, there is no elaboration on the meaning of the number. Clicking it, however, takes the visitor directly to the declaration and a form which the visitor can fill out in order to be placed on the list of signers. Most of the various language editions of *The Epoch Times*, have the form, which says, "I declare that I solemnly denounce the communist party and its affiliated organizations" (我声明 n.d., para. 5). Provided are places for name, e-mail address, location, subject, number of people represented, and comments. Below the form is the list of people who have already signed and their comments.

On the Chinese version of *The Epoch Times*, the number is prominently centered at the top of the page in a font size about three times that of the surrounding text. The several English language versions of *the Epoch Times* all feature the count of signers, but the number is centered half-way down the page and the font size is about equal to surrounding text. The number is treated as news: "Over 35,181,821 People Renounce the CCP." Under that one line, however, is a link that reads "Read the *Nine Commentaries on the Communist Party*." Clicking it, the visitor is taken to another FLG site (http:// nine commentaries.com), dedicated to the commentaries, which also includes a link for signing the declaration.

*The Epoch Times* sites are far from mere translations of the Chinese or English sites. For example, the Russian site has a banner with the number in red and color photos of Russian and Chinese Communist Party abuses (http://www.epochtimes.ru). There are also links to the *Nine Commentaries* in Russian, to the declaration against communist organizations and to the form for adding one's own name and comments to the list. The Russian document denounces communist organizations, thus including Russia's communist party, not just the Chinese Communist Party.

Several other sites leave signing the declaration more difficult. For example, on the Romanian site (http://www.epochtimes-romania.com), an animated text banner links to *The Nine Commentaries* in Romanian. The link to the declaration, however, is to the form on the English site. At the bottom of the page, there are links to the German and French sites. Perhaps, the assumption is that most Romanians function well enough in German, French or English.

The Japanese site (http://jp.epochtimes.com) shows the number of signers in two locations with a link to the *Commentaries* in Japanese. Oddly, there is no Japanese form to sign. There is, however, a link to the Chinese form on the Chinese site. Again, perhaps this tactic is a mere oversight, or perhaps it is felt that most Japanese can function well enough to navigate the Chinese site.

Any Indonesian or Swede wishing to denounce communism would find signing the form more difficult because neither the Indonesian nor the Swedish sites even provide a link (http://www.erabaru.or.id; http://www. epochtimes.se). Most surprising of all is the Vietnamese site (http://www. daikynguyen.com) which provides no references to the *Commentaries* or to the denunciation form. Perhaps this is a mere oversight, as webmasters are volunteers. Or perhaps it is an attempt to keep FLG from becoming as much an opprobrium in Vietnam as it is to the Chinese regime. For though FLG is not legal in Vietnam, the movement is not persecuted.

Regardless of the aberrations among the various *Epoch Times* sites, most of them lead to the commentaries and to the form to sign. In order to sign, however, some interested parties need to be Internet savvy and be able to navigate foreign language sites. Scanning the entries does indeed show that people of various language backgrounds are resigning from or denouncing communist organizations.

The most frequented *Epoch Times* sites are the English and the Chinese ones. Hence a comparison between the two declarations is instructive.

The English form (http://declaration.epochtimes.com) declares that up to 40,000 people each day have been renouncing the Chinese Communist Party and that the freedom and democracy movement is gaining momentum. Furthermore, the great numbers of withdrawals and declarations were triggered by the publication of the *Nine Commentaries on the Communist Party* published by *The Epoch Times*. Finally, the visitor is told: "You can participate. By submitting the form below, you can declare your position against the CCP and its harmful nature" (para 4). The English form is merely political, with no spiritual angle, and no quotations from Master Li.

The flavor of the Chinese page (http://tuidang.epochtimes.com/), however, is quite different from the English. The top left column of the page begins with a statement made by Li Hong Zhi when he signed the form, distancing himself from the CCP:

> Years ago in my work unit, everyone had to be a Chinese Communist Party member, so I passively joined. Though I never took the matter seriously. The membership expired decades ago, and I am no longer a member. But I still want to make a declaration to renounce the Chinese Communist Party. This is not for God, but for people to see. (2006, para. 1)

It must be noted, though, that the reference to God is not the only spiritualization in the text. Li signs the statement "Dafa: Li Hong Zhi" (Zhi, 2006, para. 2). As Dafa is the great law, this closing may be implying that Li is in accordance with Dafa. It might also imply that Li Hong Zhi is the Dafa. In any case, this closing is spiritual. Below Li's statement, links to the *Nine Commentaries* —a history that paints communism in China as evil and demonic—are intended to remove any hesitation people might have in signing the form.

Exclusively spiritual in thrust is the right column of the page, which begins as a letter explaining the purpose of the declaration form to the Chinese people:

> To the great Chinese people:
>
> The end of the Chinese Communist Party is near. This evil party [or evil religion] has committed great sins against people and God-Buddha in history. God will judge this devil.
>
> If one day, God appoints someone [human implied] to judge the Chinese Communist Party, they will not exclude those so-called royal Chinese Communist Party evil members. We declare solemnly that anyone who has joined the Chinese Communist Party or other organization with the Chinese Communist Party (those with the mark of the evil beast), renounce Chinese Communist Party and erase the evil marks. Once someone has judged the Chinese Communist Party, the stored record from the Epoch Times can testify for your renouncing of Chinese Communist Party.

The great law of heaven is extensive. Good and evil is distinguishable. The end of suffering, life and death is just a matter of thought. Whoever was deceived by the evil religion and whoever has born the mark of the evil beast, please grasp this great and fleeting opportunity. (Zhi, 2006, para. 1-4)

In short, based on the wording of the Chinese and English pages, the assumption seems to be that signing the declaration is a political and/or spiritual act. For English speakers, the language of the page is basically political, for Chinese speakers, clearly both political and spiritual. Both declarations, at the very least, claim that the Chinese Communist Party has violated basic human rights. But why is the spiritual element missing from the English declaration? The only explanation seems to be that English speakers are not expected to embrace the FLG cosmology. The developers of the denunciation pages clearly accept signatures as long as they denounce communism—a specific spiritual commitment is not required. This fact does not necessarily imply that the focus of FLG is political. It may simply mean that the need to stop communism is so great that any help is acceptable.

Regardless of cosmological differences, *The Epoch Times* is pleased to add more names to the list. The more names, the more the denunciation becomes an effective petition the whole world to see. After all, if the list genuinely represents over 47 million people, the FLG's demand for change in China is hard to ignore.

## POLITICAL PRESSURE AND
## NETWORKING WITH OTHER GROUPS

The FLG relies, not only on their own networks but also coordinates with other groups. For example, working with a number of human rights organizations and religious groups, FLG practitioners participate in a new form of protest against China—the human rights torch. While runners carry the Olympic torch to Beijing for the 2008 Olympic Games, other runners are carrying the human rights torch around the world and receiving an equal or greater amount of press as the Olympic torch. Not only is the human rights torch well received by activists and the media, but political figures and governmental bodies add their voice for change in China. (Proclamations, 2008)

### Lawsuits

FLG practitioners are bringing charges and lawsuits against China's government officials for various crimes. For example, in 2001, Zhao Zhifei, the Chief of the Public Security Office in Hubei Province was convicted of torture and crimes against humanity. (Table of lawsuits, 2004) More recently, in Australia, Mr. Pan Yu, a FLG practitioner, won a case against Bo Xilai, the Chinese Minister of Commerce, for torture. (Luona & Xinyu, 2007) There are at least 15 more cases underway against China officials in the courts of the United Nations Committee Against Torture, the International Criminal Court, the United Nations Human Rights Committee, the USA, Germany, Cyprus, the UK, Poland, Russia, France, Switzerland, Tanzania, Belgium, Taiwan, Finland, Armenia, Moldova, Iceland, Spain, South Korea, Indonesia and Canada. And cases against former President of China, Jiang Zemin have been filed in the USA, Belgium, Spain, Taiwan, Germany, South Korea and Greece for genocide, torture, and crimes against humanity. (Table of lawsuits, 2004).

## Reports before Governments

FLG supporters take action by asking government agencies in various countries to take action against China's persecution. For example, in September 2004, Alan Adler, the Executive Director, of Friends of Falun Gong USA testified before the United States Senate subcommittee on Immigration, Border Security And Citizenship. (Refugees, 2004)

Another way the FLG appeals for governmental support is through rallies and demonstrations. For example, in 2006 on Parliament Hill in Ottawa, where members of the Canadian Parliament turned out to support the Falun Gong in condemning the CCP's live organ harvesting. Aside from speeches and networking, practitioners put on dramas depicting organ removal from live victims, a practice reported to be actually happening in China. Those who attended included:

> one of the authors of the independent investigation report David Kilgour, MP Irwin Cotler, former Minister of Justice and Attorney General of Canada, MP Keith Martin, official opposition critic of foreign affairs, MP Wayne Marston, New Democratic Party foreign affairs critic, and MPs Larry Bagnell, Libby Davies, Diane Bourgeois, Jim Peterson and Peter Julian. (Zhi, 2006)

The above examples clearly show FLG activists attempting to influence western governments to put pressure on China to change its policy of eradicating FLG and persecuting its followers. Such activity is consistent with those of lobbies and interest groups—political activity. Nevertheless, to label FLG as a political group is to ignore the fact that FLG has no affiliations with a political party, has not supported any candidate for office and has not attempted to promote its religion in the political arena—something that cannot be said for most other popular religions, civil rights groups and humanitarian groups in America.

## SUMMARY OF CHAPTER 5

In this chapter, I discussed how Falun Gong media describe and support socialization. As in Chapter 4, the same themes arise: meditation in public parks, sharing and volunteerism, traditional and modern media, global digital networks, shows and demonstrations, digital guerilla activity, and weekend schools for children. A number of other strategies arise as well—parades, writing messages on money, texting, marketing, lobbying for political pressure, and lawsuits. The unifying central theme, however, remains constant—truthfulness, compassion and tolerance. The next chapter will discuss the Ming Hui School and the themes that arose from the Ming Hui School website, particularly in regard to goals, objectives, content and teaching methodology.

*Chapter Six*

# Ming Hui School

## THE MING HUI NETWORK

In this chapter, I discuss the Ming Hui School and the themes that arose from the Ming Hui School website, particularly in regard to how its goals, objectives, content and teaching methodology support socialization of the young.

The Los Angeles area Ming Hui School is one of many such schools around the world where FLG has begun to grow. Just as practice sites spring up in a grass-roots manner, so do local Ming Hui Schools. The impetus to start and run a Ming Hui School begins with a felt need among local practitioners, first to meet the needs of practitioner's children and also as an outreach to the local community—again the same theme of growth and conversion. And as with other FLG projects, the Ming Hui School runs off of volunteer labor.

Those interested in starting a Ming Hui School need only to take ownership of the project. Materials and help are available through the FLG network, particularly the Ming Hui School's Internet site (www.Minghui-school. org)—not to be confused with another FLG site (www.minghui.org), which is more general in nature. Indeed, beginning a Ming Hui School would not be terribly difficult with all the online help, which includes downloadable curriculum and discussion boards.

Furthermore, whenever teachers of Ming Hui Schools are unclear how to proceed, they can ask Li Hongzhi. Unlike the American homeschooling movement, which has no recognized head, FLG's founder, Li Hongzhi, is still incarnated, still at hand to settle disagreements over goals and methodology and can provide direction and encouragement over the Internet or through question and answer sessions at FLG conferences. For example, in the Washington D.C. conference in 2003, Li answered a practitioner's question about how to teach art to children; such classes should "draw things about *Dafa*" (H. Li, 2007, p. 143). In the Atlanta conference in 2003, Li answered another practitioner's question about how to teach Chinese to adult Westerners. He said to "[use] *Falun Gong*" (p. 176), the book, not *Zhuan Falun*. In New York in 2004, Li said Ming Hui Schools "shouldn't be selective about admission" (p. 218).

This chapter will analyze themes arising from the Ming Hui School website, particularly in regard to goals, objectives, content and teaching methodology. The entire curriculum is complementary to the goals of the movement. The technologies chosen facilitate communication among teachers and parents locally and globally. Furthermore, though there is a variety of subjects studied, lesson plans follow a standard pattern across the curriculum, employing ancient and contemporary techniques. Taken together, these techniques support both mastery and internalization of the content.

## THE MING HUI COMPLEMENTARY CURRICULUM

The Ming Hui School's curriculum is complementary to FLG in that the overall goals, objectives, content and methodology all fit the culture of the movement: its values, content, practices and goals. Values are based directly on Master Li's teaching. Content is adopted from Master Li's writings and from traditional cultural sources that fit, or are made to fit, Master Li's teaching. Methodology, too, fits FLG practice, but also adopts traditional Chinese practices where they are complimentary. Finally, modern instructional practices, too, are adopted from western culture. Hence, the Ming Hui School combines traditional cultural techniques, western cultural techniques and FLG techniques.

## THE MING HUI SCHOOL SITE

The vast Ming Hui School site (http://www.minghui-school.org/school /school. htm) links to numerous types of material, such as good thoughts and acts, insights regarding the practice of FLG, personal stories, school events, fairy tales and fables, literature, art, discovery of new knowledge, history and origins, downloadable radio and video programs, downloadable lesson plans.

Perhaps the most striking feature of the main page is the numerous photos from Ming Hui Schools around the world. Children and teachers, most of East Asian extraction, are seen doing various activities, from meditating in parks, to making crafts, to putting on performances. Each photo describes what they are doing and where they are. Some even include teacher contact information.

As one begins to read the buttons linking to other pages, the variety and vastness of freely available material is astounding. For example, there is a language learning page (三十六計, 2008) the content of which comes from Taiwan's Overseas Compatriot Affairs Commission (http://www.ocac.gov. tw), which provides short stories from ancient history. These stories include flash video with text read karaoke style, animation, and English translation. FLG produced content includes downloadable videos of cartoons, puppet shows and testimonies linked from NDTV (九集電視, 2008). Some of the more colorful types of content includes downloadable songs (歌曲, 2008) about FLG, successful practitioners, and even one criticizing Jiang Zemin for persecuting religion at Tiananmen in 1989. One of the most clearly useful features available from the main page is a bulletin board (明慧學校交流園地, 2008) which acts as a forum for teachers and parents to share ideas. With characteristic FLG openness, any guest may read this forum, as there is no password protection.


## SAMPLE LESSON PLAN

Lesson 19 is a typical lesson plan at the Ming Hui School integrates a number of elements (孔融讓梨, 2003). For convenience, the features of the lesson—provided from a translation on another FLG site—are provided below:

> Ming Hui School Lesson Plan: (1) Kong Rong Offering Pears
> Teaching Material Category: Ancient Story
> Selection Title: Kong Rong Offering Pears
> Target Audience: Primary School Children in Lower Grades
> Teaching Period: One Hour (Kong  Rong, 2003, para. 1)

The title of the lesson is also the title of the story from which the lesson is derived—"Kong Rong Offering Pears"—the story of a child who does not take the largest pear when offered but takes a smaller one, showing respect to his older brother and kindness to his younger brother. The story is categorized as ancient, a category from which much of FLG culture is derived. Indeed, Kong Rong is a well-known personage from the Three Kingdoms period of ancient China (A.D. 220-280), and the anecdote about the pears is mentioned in the *Three Character Classic*, which has been used in the education of children since the Song Dynasty, also used in the Ming Hui School, but which has come into disuse during the 20th century.

The plan makes clear the target audience, the lower grades of primary school. The age of the learner matches the story, which alleges that Kong

Rong was only four years old. The overall plan is ambitious, as in one hour, the teacher will narrate the story; the students will read the story aloud; they will act out the story; then, they will discuss it. And finally apply the lesson to their own lives. This format provides lots of repetition, which aids language learning as well as traditional values.

The text of the story is already in drama format, which, of course, can be read, but, more importantly, does not need to be transformed, allowing the students to focus on getting into character and learning the lessons of the story.

The aim of lesson is twofold: first, to "guide children to put others first and be willing to consider others in all respects; and second, "to be aware of the importance of cultivating courtesy in speech" (Kong Rong, 2003, para. 2).

Pears, of course, are a desirable fruit. Giving up an opportunity to take the largest requires denying oneself pleasure in order to allow someone else that pleasure. Such a theme is double edged. Foregoing pleasure fits with the FLG emphasis on tolerance—focusing on one's own character. Further, denying self for the benefit of the older brother fits with the Confucian principle, which FLG embraces, of honoring one's elders. Finally, saving the better choice for the younger brother fits with concern for those below one's level.

A five minute introduction to the lesson begins with asking the students if they have heard of Kong Rong, how old he was, and why he picked the smallest pear. One might wonder if this type of introduction spoils the story before it is even presented. In fact, it draws attention to important facts within the story which drive toward the real lesson—internalizing the moral values of young Kong Rong. Indeed, that is the story's value, not the intricacy of its plot.

Next, the teacher reads the story to the children and the students repeat in unison—a standard practice in Chinese elementary education. Again this provides repetition—time on task. The plan notes that this should take about 15 minutes. Afterward, the students are invited to perform in front of their peers—another 15 minutes. Performing aids internalization as the student has moved from group to self.

Finally, the last 15 minutes focuses on discussion. The teacher asks what the students have learned from the story. She asks them to describe the common courtesies they do every day. She asks why they should consider others first and whether they feel happy when they do so. At this point, the law of loss and gain should be brought out. And with this in mind, she prompts students to consider what other common courtesies they should employ. The final application is where the students are encouraged to assess themselves and fill out their own progress chart.

The above lesson plan is representative of lesson plans for the Ming Hui School. Lesson plans are categorized, focused on a target audience, begin with directed questions, move to reading in unison, and then drama, discussion, personal application, and self assessment.

## MING HUI CONTENT

### Myth and Legend

The Ming Hui School uses traditional stories to develop the world view of the student. For example, lesson 26 (女媧, 2004) capitalizes on the ancient and well known myth of *Nǚwā* (女媧), who repaired the sky, and created animals and humans. The story may be summarized as follows:

> When two powerful gods were quarrelling, the water god against a pillar that held up the sky causing disaster below. *Nǚwā* used a giant tortoise's legs in place of the pillar and sealed the broken sky with five colored stones (or a stone of five colors, depending on the interpretation).
> *Nǚwā* felt lonely, so she created chickens one day, dogs the next day, and so on, creating sheep, pigs, cows, and horses. Finally, she sculpted humans, who became the nobles, from yellow clay one by one until she grew tired. Then she took a rope and scattered the clay around, thus, creating lower classes (女媧, 2004).

Though most modern readers would regard *Nǚwā* as mythological, the Ming Hui School lesson treats it as historical, not unlike the Fundamentalist and Evangelical Christian approach to the Biblical account of creation.

Following the same format of introduction, repetition, drama, application and self-assessment, the lesson is a creation story, explaining how the first humans were made from yellow mud. The teacher encourages students to compare the explanation in Darwinian evolution with this particular version of intelligent design. The conclusion is that intelligent design is more believable.

Much more can be done with the story, in terms of development of the student's character. For example, one ought to emulate *Nǚwā's* example of saving the world. Or one might be reminded that the best way to solve problems is to develop one's own godlike character. *Nǚwā's* power, of course, came from her *gong*, which the student can develop through FLG.

### History

Lesson 46 (梁淑萍, 2005) is a representative example of a Ming Hui history lesson. This particular lesson is an overview of the key events during the Ming Dynasty. Historical figures of particular note are Liú Bówēn (劉伯溫), Zhèng Hé (鄭和), Hǎi Ruì (海瑞) and *Lǐ Shízhēn* (李時珍).

Zhèng Hé and *Lǐ Shízhēn* are examples of professional excellence in ancient China. Zheng He is a famed admiral whose seven expeditions took his convoy to numerous Southeast Asian locations, India, the Persian Gulf, Arabia, and to what is now Kenya—farther than any other known explorer previously. Unfortunately, after Zhèng Hé returns from the seventh voyage, the emperor decided that China was self-sufficient, having no need of foreign trade and foreign ideas. Indeed, the great seagoing ships were left to rot and the documents and maps were destroyed.

The work of *Lǐ Shízhēn*, *Běncǎo Gāng Mù* (本草綱目), completed in A.D. 1578, was a compendium of all the *materia medica* of his day. Practitioners of Chinese medicine refer to the *Běncǎo Gāng Mù* to this day. Indeed, the worldwide popularity of Chinese medicine is growing, even among purveyors of western medicine.

Liú Bówēn and Hǎi Ruì, however, provide much more fodder for moral discussion. The righteous official Hǎi Ruì was sentenced to death when he criticized the emperor for ignoring his imperial duty. Unafraid, Hǎi Ruì buys a coffin awaiting execution. The minister Xú Jiē (徐階) was able to persuade the emperor to spare Hǎi. This kindness did not stop Hǎi from prosecuting Xú's son, who was corrupt and violent. Unwilling to take bribes, Hǎi died in office, so poor that his friends had to collect money to bury him. Thus, Hǎi is remembered as an incorruptible official.

*Liú Bówēn*, one of the advisors who helped (Zhū Yuán Zhāng, 朱元璋, aka Míng Tài Zǔ, 明太祖) to established the Ming dynasty, is attributed to be the author of *shāo bǐng gē* (燒餅歌), a song about a baked cake. The song is purportedly prophetic, predicting the fall of the Ming, the rise of the Ching, as well as the later Nationalist and Communist regimes.

The story goes that Zhū Yuán Zhāng had just taken a bite of *shāo bǐng* when Liu came in for an audience. Zhū Yuán Zhāng covered up the cake and asked if Liu could guess what was on the plate. When Liu answered correctly, Zhū Yuán Zhāng asked Liu about the future of the Ming Dynasty. Liu invented the rice cake song to hide the real meaning of the prophecy, saying that the Ming would last for ten thousand sons and grandsons. What actually happened was that the grandson of Emperor Wàn Lì (萬曆, 10,000 years), *Zhū Yóu Jiǎn* (朱由檢; aka *Míng Sī Zōng,* 明思宗) became the last Ming emperor. So, in a way, Liu was right. After the grandson of Wàn Lì, the Ming dynasty was over. Liu's cryptic prediction kept him out of trouble with the emperor and foretold the fall of the Ming.

Though Liu was a great military strategist and a prophet, still he was framed numerous times by his enemies at court. The Ming Hui teacher informs the students that this is not a contradiction. Rather, telling the future is not for one's own benefit, but for determining the mandate of heaven

(天命, Tiān Mìng)—who is the legitimate ruler based on the command of Heaven (God).

Overall, the lesson covers a lot of historical ground. The most clear-cut parts of the history are the contribution of Zheng He and Lǐ Shízhēn. The stories of Hǎi Ruì and Liu Bo Wen, however, require moral judgment of political leadership, which will necessarily be based on truthfulness, compassion and tolerance.

For discussion, the teacher asks the students whether the song could predict current events. An attempt to do so is made by comparing recent history to the words of the song. A critique of the lesson, however, might be that elementary students are ill-equipped to assimilate and weigh the events of the Ming dynasty. Indeed, such history tends to be studied only by specialists in college and above. Furthermore, the song is sufficiently nebulous as to be doubtful as to its predictive ability—much like the predictions of Nostradamus.

Regardless of whether the song is predictive, the characters and the events of the stories illustrate how, in the FLG worldview, the successes of ancient China are linked to high moral standards, and the fall of ancient dynasties are linked to their moral decline. With aid from the teacher, the students may have enough familiarity with current problems in China to consider whether the mandate of heaven has passed from the present regime—the Chinese Communist Party.

## Poetry and Drawing

The two lessons discussed below are by same author, *Bú Huò* (不惑, literally "not confused"). This penname comes from a statement Confucius made about his own development:

> At fifteen I set my heart upon learning. At thirty, I had planted my feet firm upon the ground. At forty, I no longer suffered from perplexities [不惑]. At fifty, I knew what were the biddings of Heaven. At sixty, I heard them with docile ear. At seventy, I could follow the dictates of my own heart; for what I desired no longer overstepped the boundaries of right (Waley, 1956, p. 88).

What is interesting is that on the Ming Hui School site, these two lessons seem to be the only ones by this author. One might wonder why poetry and drawing are the only genera to which this author has contributed. Perhaps the key is located partly in the penname (which declares, *"I am no longer confused"*) partly in the genera and partly in the nature of FLG. Truth, of course, is the cure for confusion. And in FLG, truth is a primary value. Indeed, the names of a number of FLG websites are synonyms for truth: www.clearharmony.net, www.pureinsight.org, www.clearwisdom.net—even Minghui means *"clear wisdom."* Further, a key understanding of truth, as far as FLG is concerned is that it applies to everything, for it is a law of the universe. Hence, combining poetry with drawing is natural.

Lesson 17 (不惑, 2003a) illustrates how poetry plays a cognitive role in the Ming Hui curriculum. The poem describes the experience of practitioners doing exercises beside a beautiful lake. This lesson juxtaposes the beauty of nature and the public practice of FLG. The teacher asks the students if they have been to the lake and, if so, to describe it. Like the lessons described above, this lesson includes reading, discussion and self-examination. One difference is that this lesson includes recitation and repetition. Recitation and repetition are traditional methods of internalizing the message of poetry as well as language structures. Perhaps, more importantly, the lesson includes a meditation on how easy it is to confuse a practitioner with the yellow flowers beside the lake—oneness with nature.

Picking up where the last lesson left off, Lesson 18 (不惑, 2003b) takes the same poem as the subject of a drawing lesson. After reading aloud, students draw the scenery described in the poem. Thus, this lesson is calculated to maximize an experience of the FLG worldview.

## Science

The Ming Hui School approach to science, Lesson 35 (高雄明慧學校, 2005), includes the story of a polygraph expert who connects his equipment to plants. When the plant is being watered, the graph resembles the response of humans to pleasure. A follow-up story is of a Tang Dynasty Buddhist monk who communicated with plants. The discussion questions ask whether the students will still pick flowers, since flowers have feeling and whether it is possible to develop the ability to communicate with plants. The objective is to realize that plants have spirits too and, as always, to encourage students to do good (have compassion).

Lesson 12 (鍾俊妃, 2003), addresses both science and culture. The lesson begins with the traditional Moon Festival and a fable surrounding it. It also introduces classic poems describing the beauty of the full moon. Finally, the lesson introduces the real origin of the moon; according to Master Li, humans put it there long ago. Though such technology has been long lost, it is now being regained through FLG.

## MING HUI METHODOLOGY

### Modern Methods

In the chapter on FLG media, much has already been said about how the FLG networks using the Internet. This is true of the Ming Hui School's vast website, which also links to other FLG websites. The fact that the Ming Hui School relies so heavily on the Internet cannot be ignored, especially in light of the fact that the Internet is both a modern and a western technology. Only recently has such technology been ubiquitous and thus available to new movements.

## Stories and Drama

As has been noted, every lesson includes drama. But it should also be observed that every lesson includes a story, whether historical, legend, myth, drawing, crafts or music. Even science lessons include a story. From the story, drama arises. And from the drama, internalization begins to take place.

## Teaching Methodology

Considering the vast amount and variety of materials and methods used by the Ming Hui School, there is little mention of a philosophy of education or methodology. There is, of course, regular reference to Master Li's teaching and FLG, from which a general approach seems to have taken form. One practitioner describes the philosophy of education thus:

> The responsibility of creating a new age for the mankind might rely on the children's shoulders. We believe that an education based on cultivating the students' morality is genuine education for humankind. This is the education philosophy of Minghui School. (Young practitioners' tales, 2005, para. 2)

Thus, the Ming Hui School philosophy of education centers on instilling morality in children, who will create a new age—the new vision of the future.

## Multiple Intelligences

Though no educational theory seems to be employed, the practices of the Ming Hui School do resemble present Western educational practice. For example, without prior knowledge of Gardner's Multiple Intelligences theory (Gardner, 1999), the Ming Hui lessons consistently develop each of the domains. The Ming Hui School's stress on concern for others is an interpersonal focus. Similarly, the regular self-evaluation is an intrapersonal focus. The consistent instruction in Chinese is a linguistic concern. The dramas and, to some extent, the meditations are bodily-kinesthetic interests. Appreciation of music and nature is built into many lessons. Finally, there is a regular appeal to logic—though outsiders might find the logic questionable as it is not always linear. The only intelligence that does not seem to be stressed is spatial. Nevertheless, spatial intelligence may be shown as integrated with other intelligences (such as the bodily-kinesthetic) to produce drama.

Whether the use of these different intelligences results of interaction with Western educational theory, comes from the practice of FLG, or somewhere else, is uncertain. Yet it is clear that regular employment of these intelligences is not standard in Chinese culture.

## Metacognition and Self-Assessment

Self-assessment has never been a feature of Chinese education. The teacher has always been the primary source for feedback. Yet the regular self-assessment incorporated within the Ming Hui School lessons matches a western theory of development which has been slowly, very slowly, gaining acceptance (Flavell, 1979).

## Traditional Method: Memorization

As was shown in the lessons requiring recitation, memorization is a method which FLG employs. Students memorize ancient poems, as well as portions of Master Li's writing. Though the west long abandoned memorization, and though FLG seems to have adopted western techniques, the time honored tradition of memorization continues. The combination of ancient and modern techniques may add vitality to the overall learning experience.

## Spirituality

Transmission. Though much of the discussion, so far, has elaborated on the interactive and creative nature of education in the Ming Hui School, which implies a child-centered approach, other features of the Ming Hui approach must also be kept in mind: memorization and recitation of texts, and conformity to truthfulness, compassion and tolerance. This implies a transmission approach to education.

Indeed, the idea of transmission is not limited to knowledge, or even to worldview. Transmission takes place in a spiritual dimension. Master Li explains:

> I can reassure you now—every student has my Law Body behind him, and not just one. So my Law Bodies will do those things. When you teach someone he'll get a Law Wheel right then and there if he has the karmic relationship for it. If he has less of a karmic relationship, after his body is rebalanced he'll slowly come to get a Law Wheel through practicing, and my Law Bodies will help him rebalance his body. (H. Li, 2003, p. 70)

Thus, teaching the *Fa* brings Master Li's Law Bodies, which aid in the transformation of the whole character. Indeed, Master Li, himself, used the phrase "transmitting the Law" (H. Li, 2003, p. 193) in reference to teaching the law.

Reception. In educational circles, the primary criticism of transmission as a methodology is that it is not well received and thus is ineffective. When teachers transmit (as in a lecture), the student either does not understand, quickly forgets or even rejects the message. The Ming Hui School, indeed, FLG in general, seems to have avoided this problem either by using a variety of methods or by the spiritual power behind the transmission itself.

One might suggest that the student's belief in the spiritual efficacy of FLG is the reason for the social, emotional and physical changes experienced by the student. Regardless of whether the power of FLG is real, the method seems to work for many. Indeed, students report an altered sense of perception.

New vision. Aside from the many accounts of how a student's character has improved, children are reported as having visions. One such account is of a war in other dimensions. The child saw demons trying to possess people's bodies, "the universe full of Faluns cleaning up demons" (What Shanshan Saw, 2001, para. 3). She also saw a number of gods Buddhas and Taos doing battle with the demons, and she describes the end of those who hate Dafa, "When their spirits left their bodies, they were already aware of everything and felt endless pain and extreme grief . . . .seconds after they left their bodies, their spirits were sucked in and dissolved by the Flaming Red Sphere" (What Shanshan saw, 2001, para. 15) on which was written truthfulness, compassion and tolerance. Visions such as these, derived from FLG teaching, are evidence that the new worldview has taken root deep within the psyche.

## SUMMARY OF CHAPTER 6

In this chapter, I discussed the themes arising from the Ming Hui School website, particularly in regard to goals, objectives, content and methodology. The school was found to have a regular regimen of directed questions, reading in unison, drama, discussion, personal application, and self assessment. Content included myth and legend, history, poetry and drawing, science, stories and drama. Overall methods were eclectic, resembling techniques stemming from Multiple Intelligences theory and Metacognition theory. Traditional techniques were used as well: memorization, transmission, and meditation—with evidence of visions occurring. The next chapter will compare the Ming Hui School with three different weekend schools, whose cultural groups, in some way, intend to supplement the curriculum of the public schools.

*Chapter Seven*

# Comparing Ming Hui
# with Similar Schools

As the educational approach of the Ming Hui School flows from the culture of the FLG movement, one might wonder in what ways and to what extent the approaches of similar schools would fit their movements. With this question in mind, I did some preliminary investigation into three other schools. The primary criteria were that the school should be in the Los Angeles area and that the school should be taking something thought of as the paternity of one culture and making it universally available. Of interest would be the following:

> What is the culture?
> Why should it be taught?
> How should it be taught?
> What success does the school purport to have achieved?

The very nature of these questions could indeed generate another complete study, which would likely be quite revealing. Nevertheless, the intent of this chapter is only to describe the extent to which these movements match the hallmarks already observed in the FLG movement, not to analyze these schools in detail.

## LOS ANGELES AREA CHINESE SCHOOL

Los Angeles Area Chinese School (Actual names have been changed for the sake of confidentiality) is largely a standalone school for children. However, it is affiliated with the larger Los Angeles Area Chinese Culture Association of Southern California and networks with local public schools. According to its mission statement, "The mission of the [School] is to provide Chinese language education and to promote Chinese culture to interested individuals in the community." Unlike FLG, Los Angeles Area Chinese School does not seem to have a moral agenda. There is no rhetoric about the need to "save" anyone, no transformation of mind, body or culture, no plan for world expansion.

The membership directory and the website shows bias—though perhaps unintentional—against non-Chinese. For example, there was one photo of a non-Chinese in a directory full of photos of classes in progress. Only two class descriptions included a language other than Chinese. Further, the website offers virtually no information without a password to enter. Both the directory and the website provide contact information in English which may ultimately produce a password, but one might wonder whether the uninitiated would contact a seemingly closed group. Hence, the methods being used perpetuate the Chinese language and culture among the Chinese.

The curriculum "uses textbooks from Taiwan, China and the US based on traditional and simplified Chinese characters." Hence, there would be little use of ancient texts or ancient methods of instruction. There seems to be no bias as to the origin of the materials, except, perhaps, on the part of the children. Indeed, one teacher from the school told me that the children tend to prefer using the *pinyin* over the *zhuyin* transliteration system, as the former resembles English and is therefore easier to learn.

According to the Table of Contents, there are only four types of course offerings: Chinese language for children, *Taichi*, line dance and tennis. Hence, 50% of the activities offered (line dance and tennis) are unrelated to Chinese culture. Perhaps the best way to understand the offerings is an opportunity for the local Chinese community to have fellowship. Indeed, photos of a carnival and what appears to be a talent show suggest a fun time of Chinese food and games.

Los Angeles Area Chinese School is nonprofit and students may be able to earn "10 credits per school year toward college." Tuition is low, and subsidized, but not free. Indeed, students who drop out will receive a prorated portion of their tuition.

Los Angeles Area Chinese School is quite different from the Ming Hui School. In Ming Hui, all materials and methods relate directly to the target culture. The materials and methods come in great variety and color. Everything is freely given without charge. Donations by nonmembers are not accepted. Los Angeles Area Chinese School, on the other hand, does "accept donations to replace, purchase equipment, or set up new programs" while still charging for materials and teaching. That which is provided for free, the membership directory and limited access to the website, are largely monochrome. Growth and development do not seem to be a driving force at all. Indeed, there seems to be no controlling philosophy, no specific methodology, and no statement about the nature of Chinese culture or the reason for preserving it or sharing it.

## A SATURDAY KOREAN SCHOOL

Hope Korean Church (Actual names have been changed for the sake of confidentiality) in the Los Angeles area, with a membership exceeding 3,500, provides four hours of instruction in Korean language and culture for children in the community every Saturday. The school has been in existence for four years and currently enrolls around 130 students.

In order to better understand the nature of the school, I interviewed one of the school's teachers, who explained the school's goals, methodology and content. According to the teacher, the goals of the school are to aid students to preserve the Korean language and culture and to reach out to the community. The target students are second generation Korean children. The cost of tuition is $300 per semester, which defrays the cost of the teachers' salaries.

There are three levels of instruction: preschool, grade 1 and grade 2. These three classes teach basic literacy. Starting with the Korean phonetic symbols that make up the written language, students memorize vocabulary words, sing traditional Korean children's songs with motions, play traditional Korean games and make traditional craft items, such as folding screens and paper fans. At the end of the semester, the children put on a show for their parents.

Two factors seem to be the primary reasons for the low level of growth: low goals and interference within the church itself. The stated goals are to aid Koreans to preserve their Korean language and culture and, since this is a church, "to reach out to," evangelize, the community. In part, the effectiveness of the overall program may be in question since, admittedly, few become Christians as a result of the program and most of the students, over 90%, give up the attempt to learn Korean after finishing the courses offered.

Nevertheless, that is not to say that the school is not contributing to the church's overall goal of growth. The existence of the school may be acting as the original draw. Afterward, the fact that the students have another option at the church, the English Ministry, interferes with the goal of nurturing the students' Korean language and culture. Within one church of ethnic Koreans, indeed within families, there are two separate cultural entities. The first generation, who prefer Korean, and the second generation, who prefer English. Illustrative of this cultural division is the fact that the church's Korean website and English website function completely separately. Indeed, the church's website, which is mostly in Korean, displays no link to its English ministry, and the English Ministry's website has no link to the Korean site.

Both, however, provide free downloadable texts, audio and video in their respective languages.

If the goal is indeed to promote Korean language and culture, it seems that the church and school have not found a successful approach. Whatever successes accomplished by the present classes, they dissipate without continuing classes or immersion in Korean culture. For the competing English ministry provides a satisfying mono-cultural experience. Until the school is able to provide a continuing Korean experience that is able to compete with (or at least interact with) the American culture, students will abandon their Korean roots in favor of the language and culture of the adopted country. The best the school can hope for is adoption of the Korean Christian faith and appreciation of the Korean culture, not a truly bicultural or even cross-cultural facility.


## THE KABBALAH SCHOOL: SPIRITUALITY FOR KIDS

Spirituality for Kids (SFK), founded in Los Angeles in 2001 to aid "at risk children and families from underprivileged parts of the world" (Community programs, 2006, para. 8), now conducts programs in Israel, London, Malawi, México and Panama, as well as Los Angeles, New York, and Miami. The SFK website (http://sfk.org) suggests that the phenomenal growth is directly related to the effectiveness of their curriculum and methodology. Utilizing "the best educational practices" (Curriculum, 2008, para. 1), SFK empowers "kids to overcome challenges and improve the quality of their lives and the world around them."

These sweeping claims have an authentic ring as the site shows children from a variety of religious backgrounds and races interacting happily. Indeed, the SFK site links to video YouTube videos showing children in war torn areas laughing and hugging their former "enemies" (KCP direction, 2008). The site also links to a study on the school by Rand Corporation (Maestas & Gaillot, 2008a). The study found "positive effects on virtually every domain covered by the survey" (p. 1). Furthermore, "program effects persisted at 12-week follow-up" (p. 1). It must also be noted, however, that SFK paid for and instigated the study (Maestas & Gaillot, 2008b).

With such praise, the school's approach to education deserves careful consideration. The curriculum is "based on the ideas of sharing, cause and effect and the universal human truths" (What Spirituality, 2008, para. 8). As these ideas are not new to education, what is it about the curriculum that impacts the children so deeply? In the ten weeks of the Level 1 curriculum, the "children learn that they can "win the game" and achieve their potential when they follow the "rules" (i.e., making an effort, caring for others, and making responsible choices) (Curriculum, 2008, para. 2). Again, these goals are not so out of the ordinary as to produce results head and shoulders above other programs.

In Level 2, children spend eight weeks investigating themselves by "finding clues within" (Curriculum, 2008, para. 13). Students begin to do this in Lesson one by exploring "how their own positive actions can create a constructive and happy future for themselves, their friends and family, and the world" (para. 14). How looking within aids the student in creating a happy future for the self and the entire world is not immediately clear. However, clues to the actual methodology appear through comparing the objectives of the lessons. In lesson 2, students "identify a time when they behaved reactively and brainstorm possible consequences of their behavior" (para. 15). Once the possible consequences are identified, the next lesson encourages students to "discover the staying power of words" (para. 16). How this power is discovered, is not stated. Lesson 4 students learn that it is necessary to discover what one wants and to set goals in order to "get results" (para. 17). In Lesson 5, "the children present the concepts to each other, taking an active role and caring for others' learning process" (para. 18). Clearly, the concepts are taking an active role and caring for how others learn—which, in part, explains the earlier question of how the children are taught to make themselves and the world happy. They are empowered to do this by learning how to share the light, care for others, restrict impulses, take proactive measures and practice techniques for honing concentration.

Are these disciplines the solution to improving overall student academic ability and attitudes? This is what is suggested by the stated goals and objectives of Levels 1-3. Further investigation of the site, however, reveals a hidden curriculum which is accessed through unique tools. Indeed, on one page describing SFK, the word *"tools"* occurs six times:

Spirituality For Kids teaches children the tools for life . . . tools that will help them realize their full potential and change the course for them and future generations. (What Spirituality, 2008, para.1)

[Students will] give others the same tools to write their own success stories. (para. 7)

Spirituality for Kids partners with educators, schools and organizations to teach tools to assist children in making choices to change their course and benefit future generations. (para. 9)

We've created unique tools specifically benefiting all types of learning-auditory, kinesthetic and visual. (para. 10)

The unique tools we've created specifically benefit all types of learning-auditory, kinesthetic and visual-to provide an understandable language that connects children with these universal truths. (para. 11)

What are these tools and why are they unique? Whatever these tools are, SFK suggests that they apply universal truths to unlock students' full potential and allow them to write their own success, regardless of learning style. Hence, further investigation into these tools is imperative to understanding the SFK phenomenon.

The founder of SFK is Karen Berg, "co-director and co-founder of The Kabbalah Centre International, the largest educational and spiritual organization dedicated to the teachings of this ancient but timeless wisdom" (About us, 2008, para. 1). Nor is it a mere coincidence that Karen Berg has started both organizations. The Kabbalah Centre's website lists SFK as one of its community programs. Once this is understood, it becomes clear what the tools taught at SFK are. Indeed, the oft repeated buzzword in the Kabbalah Centre materials is "tools." In *The Power of Kabbalah* by Yehuda Berg (2004), one of Karen Berg's sons, seven tools are elaborated on: imagining the Opponent whispering in your adversary's ear, the red string to ward off the "evil eye" (p. 249), blessed water, dreams, resistance without judging, possession of the *Zohar*, and meditation on the 72 names of God. These are the beliefs and practices rooted in Kabbalah that SFK teaches.

The uniqueness of SFK's teaching is not merely that it is rooted in the Kabbalah, but that it is a return to the original practice from which other Kabbalists diverged. Kabbalah is generally understood to be Jewish mystical practices—though non-Jews have practiced it—and requires a facility with Aramaic. Rabbis have traditionally taught Kabbalah only to Jewish men over 40 who are well versed in Judaism (Goldberg & Thomson). The Kabbalah Centre, however, does away with all these restrictions. Indeed, the Kabbalah Centre website has pages in Spanish, Portuguese, German, and Russian. Kabbalah Centre materials are also available for sale in these languages. Karen Berg told ABC News, "It wasn't until we started really bringing it to the people that they actually had access to this knowledge" (2005, para. 5).

Aside from whatever actual benefits students may receive from SFK, the question of how financing and publicity affects growth also should be considered. Followers and admirers alike are encouraged to donate to these nonprofit organizations. Indeed, both the Kabbalah Centre and SFK sites include a special page for donating by credit card.

Sitting under the teaching at the center is $25 per session (Ongoing lectures, 2004). Furthermore, publications also generate revenue. To name a few of the income generating products, the cost of Yehuda Berg's *Red String DVD* (2008) is $9.95; Karen Berg's *God Wears Lipstick* (2005) is $17.95; Yael Yardeni's downloadable video *Worldwide Classroom—Kabbalistic Astrology* (2008) is $150; and the Kabbalah Centre's 23 volume *Zohar* $415 (2003).

Among their most famous followers is the pop-star Madonna, whose Kaba-listic children's books, *Mr. Peabody's Apples* (Madonna & Long, 2003), *The English Roses* (Madonna & Fulvimari, 2003) and *Yakov and the Seven Thieves* (Madonna & Spirin, 2004) are sold on the site. Madonna's contributions do not end there. Indeed, she devotes several million pounds each year, besides buying the £3.6 million venue for the London organization and the £12 million Kab-balah Centre school in New York (Barnes, 2006). Madonna is even a cofounder of the Kabbalah Centre's Raising Malawi project (Luscombe, 2006).

## COMPARISON AND CONTRAST

The three schools reviewed in this chapter all have similarities to FLG in that they purport to teach a culture different from the predominant one in Southern California. All of them show some commitment to their language of origin, but the level of its importance is quite different. For the ethnic Chinese in FLG, the Chinese language is important enough for practitioners to volunteer to teach it to other practitioners' children. Indeed, the expectation is that the students will continue to use Chinese in the future, despite the fact that they are living in the United States. Promoting Chinese over other languages is not a goal, but facility with it clearly is. For mastery of Chinese provides access to the ancient texts—the source of the revitalized culture.

The Los Angeles Area Chinese School, on the other hand, shows a lan-guage curriculum for several levels, but the reason for learning Chinese de-pends wholly on the motivation of the student. Indeed, a photo of one group of students intimated that they had been together for eleven years. There is no evidence that non-Chinese are intentionally excluded, but there seems to be no attempt to bring in other ethnicities, either.

The Korean school, like the Los Angeles Area Chinese School, shows no evidence of appeal to other ethnicities. Indeed, though a fair amount of effort goes into teaching three levels of Korean classes, language acquisition is not sufficiently valued to provide more levels or to bring about interaction between the two cultural groups—regardless of the fact that lack of language facility divides this church comprised of only one ethnicity even divides its families.

The Kabbalah school (SFK), teaches profound spiritual truths springing from an understanding of Hebrew and Aramaic texts. And though knowledge of the languages is recommended, neither SFK nor the Kabbalah Centre teaches the languages of the Kabbalah. Yet doing so is unnecessary because virtually all of the materials are available in multiple languages. One scholar suggested to me that if people begin to attend the "connections" (worship services), they will learn the languages of the Kabbalah by rote.

Three of the four schools promote a spiritual practice, of which three are millenarian. Only Los Angeles Area Chinese School is not. Further, only Los Angeles Area Chinese School has no link to spiritual practices, with the possible exception of a Taichi class. SFK promotes spiritual tools that are supposed to act on principles of the universe, ultimately producing a perfect world. SFK is not supposed to be a religion, but is supposed to be compatible with any religion. The Korean school is an arm of an evangelical church, which promotes salvation through faith in Jesus Christ. As such, the Korean school is spiritual, religious and millenarian.

The Chinese school and the Korean School each remain the domain of one ethnicity. There seems to be no impetus to pursue a multi-ethnic or cross-cultural approach. Indeed, the Chinese school merely represents a way that local Chinese centers around the world have aided their own children to acquire cultural knowledge that may aid in their future success. The Korean School represents the same, though to a much lesser degree as the church's bifurcated approach to growth interferes with language acquisition.

SFK and FLG have much more in common. Both the text and the images on FLG and SFK websites are multi-ethnic and cross-cultural. What is it that induces traditionally exclusivist spiritual practices, such as FLG and Kabbalah, to open up to different ethnicities, cultures, and languages? The traditional understanding of revitalization movements is that the vision of a charismatic leader is the inspiration for creating a more satisfying culture, but this has hitherto been limited to local cultures.

A common experience between FLG and SFK is a history of persecution and violence. The Jews have been persecuted for centuries, so have the White Lotus sects. More recently, the Chinese government has been attempting to stamp out FLG. Similarly, the Kabbalah Center in Israel has experienced governmental suppression, and hordes of Orthodox Jews have marched against the Kabbalah Center in Los Angeles. The many horrors of the present-day world (inner-city violence, ethnic and religious conflicts, poverty and hunger) provide the impetus for the dream of crafting a comprehensible message of how to create a satisfying global culture. How the prophet transmits that vision to would-be followers and how followers participate in establishing the new mazeway is the subject of this study. Ancient and modern technology makes the necessary cooperation, communication and fundraising possible. And schools for children are seen as an important strategy for the success of the movement.

## SUMMARY OF CHAPTER 7

In this chapter, I compared the Ming Hui School to a community-based Chinese school, a church-based Korean school, and a Kabbalah-based school.

The Chinese school exhibited a commitment to language learning, but it showed no evidence of appealing to non-Chinese in the community. Furthermore, it showed little evidence of a deep commitment to Chinese culture and no evidence of a spiritual commitment. The Korean school exhibited a commitment to the Christian faith, but only cursory commitment, or at least limited success, to culture and language learning. The Kabbalah-based school, unlike the other two, showed both a deep commitment to spiritual practices and highly successful cross-cultural appeal. What was not evident was any commitment to language learning. Furthermore, like, Falun Gong, the Kabbalah-based school showed evidence of addressing socio-political conflict. In the next chapter, the Conclusion, I will review the results of this study and discuss how the theory that arose from the data may be of use to educators.

*Chapter Eight*

# Conclusion

As is seen in Chapter One, the FLG movement arose, at least in part, out of the *qigong* movement, which the Chinese government developed from traditional culture and introduced to the general population to help meet healthcare needs. Many perceived FLG to be the best of all the *qigong* schools and Li Hong Zhi received many honors. Later, the government believed FLG to be a threat and tried to put a stop to it through force. When FLG followers tenaciously protested, the government began a severe persecution, which has acted as an attention getter abroad and a platform for FLG. The extent to which the government has been able to squash FLG at home remains to be seen, as the practice has largely gone underground.

Chapter Two discusses the question of why such movements arise, which is answered only in part by the various theories, such as Linton's (1943) theory of nativistic movements, Wallace's (1956) revitalization movements, rational choice theory (Stark & Bainbridge, 1987), as well as other popular constructs—relative deprivation, alienation, modernization, and secularization. The most thorough of these theories is revitalization theory, as the others can easily fit inside it as variables—types of stress upon culture. In several ways, Falun Gong fits revitalization theory.

As Wallace's (1956) theory suggests, FLG is "deliberate, organized, conscious effort by members of a society to create a more satisfying culture" (p. 265). Furthermore, FLG has followed the sequential process described in the theory: steady state, stress, distortion, revitalization, steady state. The term *steady state* does not imply that the culture does not change but that change is slow. When change becomes too rapidly for the culture to adjust, revitalization movements occur.

To find the last steady state in Chinese culture, we must look back more than 150 years to the slow decline of the Qing Empire. Throughout the 19th Century, encroachments into the weak Qing Empire introduced increasing cultural stresses which brought about the Taiping Rebellion in 1850 and the Boxer movement in 1899 and finally the end of the dynastic tradition (1911) and the Republic of China (1912). Unrest continued as warlords struggled for power; then the Nationalists and Communists struggled for power. Even after Mao had firm control of the country, his philosophy was one continual revolution—plunging the country into one purge after another. After Mao's death, Deng Xiaoping rose to power and began a policy of modernizing agriculture, industry, science and technology, and national defense—the "Four Modernizations." This plan, designed to make China a great economic power by the early 21st century, has succeeded, but not without extreme stresses. Several of the world's most polluted cities are in China. Millions have little or no access to healthcare or education, and religious freedom is curtailed. All of the above illustrate rapid change and excessive stresses.

Over the 150 years sketched above, the fast cultural changes and stresses, both foreign and domestic, have bred revitalization movements—the Taiping Rebellion, the Boxer Movement, even Mao's Cultural Revolution could be described as a revitalization. All of these ultimately failed. The Taiping Rebellion and the Boxers were put down. The Cultural Revolution failed to outlast its prophet. The stresses remain.

In China, the last steady state was more than 150 years ago. Stress and distortion have produced several failed attempts at revitalization. Falun Gong represents the most recent attempt to revitalize the culture. As Wallace's theory (Wallace, 1956) predicts, FLG has a charismatic central prophet with a renewed vision of the supernatural (p. 270), including impending danger of apocalyptic world-destruction. The prophet provides rules for moral conduct which bring people back to their longed for ideal state—their true selves. The prophet preached the new message and gathered to himself disciples who have "assumed much of the responsibility for communicating the 'good word'" (p. 273). An organization developed in three orders: the prophet, the close disciples and the regular followers. And the movement developed a number of strategies for adaptation.

What was not predicted by Wallace (1956) is that one strategy could be cross-cultural growth and internationalization of the movement. What remains to be seen is whether "a controlling portion of the population" (p. 275) will ultimately accept the new religion, the routinization of the culture (it becomes established as normal) and finally a new steady state. At the time of this writing, the cultural confrontation continues.

Will FLG fail to be accepted by the majority of the culture? Will it fail to reach a steady state? The answer to these questions is contingent upon what we mean by "the population." Clearly, what Wallace intended by this phrase was the individuals within a specific locale and a specific ethnicity—or, at least, a limited set thereof. FLG exemplifies how culture crosses such boundaries. Doing so, the question must be changed: Will a controlling portion of the world accept FLG? FLG is now competing with all the world religions.

If FLG is not accepted by the majority of the world, and yet survives as an entity, what is FLG? Is FLG disqualified from being a revitalization movement simply because it cannot supplant most of the world's religions? I propose that the rules of cultural conflict have changed by the very nature of this cross-cultural dynamic.

If we allow that a revitalization movement can cross-cultures without having to be adopted by the majority of a population, how then should cultural transformation, routinization and steady state be designated? Perhaps it is best to continue to let the nature of the new culture revise the model. If local boundaries may be crossed, and all ethnicities are welcome, then the extent to which the movement is able to develop within the world community is the extent to which the movement has become routinized. Wallace's definition of a steady state may still be used: "Once a cultural transformation has been accomplished and the new cultural system has proved itself viable, and once the movement organization has solved its problems of routinization, a new steady state may be said to exist" (Wallace, 1956, p. 275).

In several ways, FLG exhibits variables hitherto not discussed in regard to revitalization. Why does the movement appeal to all levels of society? Why has it grown into an international, multi-ethnic and cross-cultural movement?

## A COMPELLING NEW VISION FOR ALL

FLG in Southern California is a marriage of ancient and modern culture. It satisfies because it reunites the present with the past, especially for Chinese practitioners, because FLG addresses nagging concerns that are not being successfully addressed through other means. FLG addresses immediate concerns of maintaining or improving health, dissatisfaction with the perceived malignant government at home (China), a feeling of having lost continuity with one's cultural roots, a feeling of moral decline (both on a personal level and society as a whole), a disenchantment with materialism (both as a philosophy and as an experience of consumerism), a feeling that the world is increasingly interconnected by geopolitics, economics and technology yet failing to meet each other's needs and, indeed, often causing harm to each other. Finally,

FLG addresses the ever nagging existential problems of the human condition and the desire for ultimate truth, hence responses such as, "This is what I've been looking for!" and "They could explain everything!"

FLG immediately addresses the health concerns, provides strategies for bringing about change in the Chinese government at home; engages in mining Chinese history for present application; restores faith that morality is both desirable and achievable; provides a plausible worldview incorporating present scientific knowledge without resorting to mere materialism; and restores the hope of successfully connecting with others, even on a global scale. Indeed, it has been shown that FLG is appealing to non-Chinese. Adopting FLG does not require becoming Chinese in any sense. It does, however, require adopting a mazeway that exhibits elements of both old China and the modern western world. And it does require its own form of thinking globally. As was shown in Chapter 2, none of the existing theories have been able to account for all of the significant features exhibited by FLG. Hence, a new term is called for—cross-cultural revitalization movement (CCRM), the characteristics of which will be developed below.

The interviews reviewed in Chapter Four and the FLG literature reviewed in Chapter Five reveal how FLG nurtures a concern for others, even outside of one's own cultural context. A CCRM must not only revitalize but make complete changes. For example, volunteerism and sharing, key themes in FLG, have not been common themes in Chinese history; though they have been part of western thought since the Enlightenment. The FLG version of sharing results in free teaching sessions, transparency in interpersonal interactions, and virtually all resources obtainable for free even without a commitment to FLG. This low cost of access appeals to anyone interested in solutions but is not yet willing to make a commitment. Similarly, age, race, ethnicity, religion, sex—the walls that usually prevent cultural change—are no hurdle for the CCRM. The reasons for this are rooted in the worldview of the founder, and hence the movement as a whole.

The tools and methods used by FLG in the socialization process are not new to the world. Public exercises, small group sharing and demonstrations are not new; nor are digital networks particularly new. Nor yet is the belief that all humans have a dignity which is rooted in the ultimate meaning of the cosmos. What is new is the combination of a broad continuum of old and new technologies and methods employed to promote and develop the new culture and vision locally and around the world.

What distinguishes FLG as a CCRM, as opposed to some other type of movement, is not simply the technology and techniques employed; it is the overall approach to their use. It is the integration of plugged in and unplugged human interaction; it is the perception that the one-to-one relationship in Taoism of master to student is now available to all; it is the encouragement of the individual to participate in any way his/her gifting allows; it is the way in which FLG is both centralized (with Li Hong Zhi as the absolute authority) and decentralized (with local groups maintaining themselves through voluntary donation of time, money, effort and creativity). It is the integration of all the above through the moral filter of truthfulness, compassion and tolerance that establishes a more satisfying culture, transforming the character of the individual and even the whole world.

With all the above in mind, it can be said that in CCRMs, doing flows from being; the how (conversion, growth, methods) flows from the what (worldview, belief). CCRMs do not lose sight of this because they are a critique of a failing system. Mazeways perish when the old worldview is no longer generally shared or when the methods have drifted so far from the ideals that the disconnect becomes unbearable. Success of a CCRM does not necessarily require all of society to embrace the new mazeway, but it does require the survival and stability of the new movement.

## MODEL OF FLG SOCIALIZATION

A model of socialization in FLG was developed based on the interrelationships among the themes arising from the data (see Figure 8.1). Adult conversion in FLG begins with an individual making a choice to investigate further or to try out FLG (see figure H1). Future studies, however, may wish to look at how children raised in FLG families and/or trained in the Ming Hui School assimilate their upbringing. Motivating factors for the adults include the health benefits of FLG, the ways practitioners share and volunteer, how practitioners in China continue to practice FLG despite persecution, and the new vision. The ways in which practitioners validate the *Fa* are numerous and have the effect of improving the practitioners' own character, as well as impacting others and the world at large. Once the choice is made to try FLG—if only to scan the literature, to listen to a story or to try out the exercises—the *Fa* begins to be validated, thus starting a process of growth. Indeed, there is no specific rite of passage.

The process of socialization tends to be described as a surprise and a satisfaction that FLG addresses the felt needs and even needs hitherto unknown. In whatever way the practitioner begins to participate, the *Fa* is being validated. The character of the individual changes from the inside. Indeed, the worldview of FLG becomes internalized so that the actions of a practitioner are desired, not required. As a practitioner reaches new levels, the desire to validate the *Fa* becomes stronger.

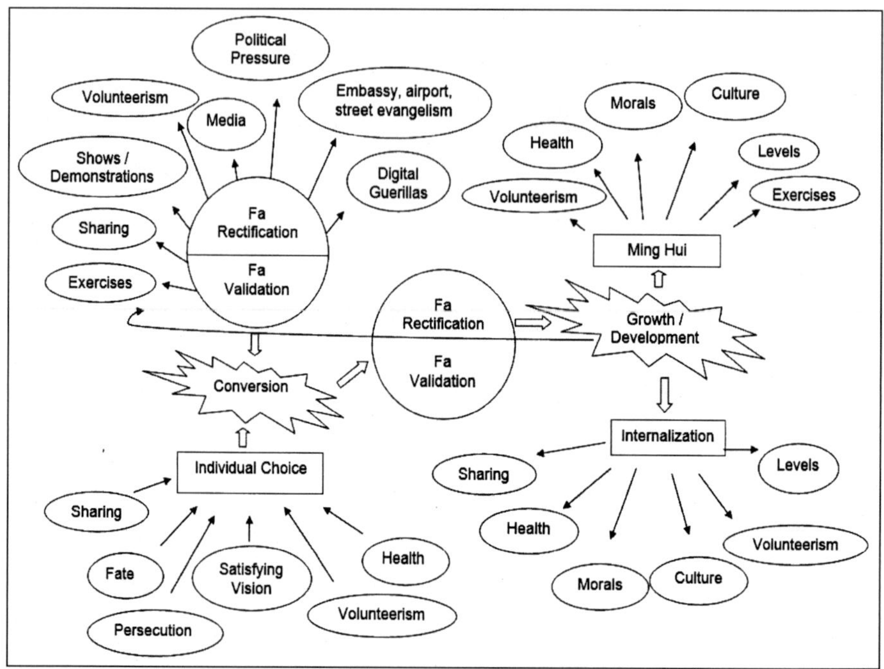


**Figure 8.1.   Socialization in Falun Gong.**

The Ming Hui School is yet another example of how to validate the *Fa*. As the children learn the exercises, volunteerism, morals, and culture, their health improves and their character level rises. Indeed, aside from whatever academic processes that take place in the Ming Hui School, the children are taught to validate the Fa, which affects themselves and the entire cosmos.

Finally, validating the *Fa* aids in both conversion and in the growth of practitioners around the world. Hence, conversion and growth interact with each other, spiraling upward to greater levels of validity. When all of these figures are put together, a complex model of FLG socialization appears.

Any model of movements must take careful consideration of the individual. Indeed, Wallace's original model notes that "individual members of a population . . . experience increasingly severe stress" (1956, p. 269) as the old mazeway fails. This is born out in FLG as a large percentage of new converts in Southern California (as well as what was seen in the FLG publications) are non-Chinese and from individualistic cultures as well as collectivistic ones. What motivates individuals to convert and to stay within a movement? They are satisfied. Furthermore, a movement is not merely made up of individuals but takes on a life of its own. This, too, must be considered. Forces outside the control of the group must be considered—economics, political processes, and other groups. For these influence how both individuals and groups make decisions and how they see the world. Nor are forces limited to that which is scientifically measurable. Spiritual forces and/or altered states of consciousness must be considered, regardless of the researcher's worldview. The focus should be the worldview of those within the movement, not the preconceptions of the researcher.

The benefit of this grounded theory methodology has been to develop a theory based on the data, not to prove the theory either locally or outside of the context of the study. Proving the theory will remain for a future study, which may even develop a better model. Meanwhile, this study suggests that FLG is a hitherto undefined type of revitalization movement: a CCRM.

That is not to say that FLG is the only CCRM. The Kabbalah Center may also prove to be one by a more thorough study. Both the Kabbalah Centre and FLG tout an ancient, unique cultivation of truth available nowhere else, which used to be passed down from master to student but is now available to all. Their socialization methods—such as volunteerism, digital networking and aiding the oppressed—are also similar.

Nevertheless, significant differences remain. The Kabbalah Centre teachers receive financial support, and obtaining the Kabbalah Centre's secret knowledge tends toward hefty investment, which may limit the Kabbalah Centre's volunteerism. It is possible, however, to take classes for "free" in exchange for volunteer activity. In contrast, no one receives reimbursement for teaching FLG. Volunteerism is the rule, not the exception. Nor is FLG the pet religion of the rich. More importantly, the Kabbalah Center movement is not facing severe persecution, but FLG is. The extent to which a movement is a CCRM, therefore, may depend on its cost to benefit ratio. For some, the Kabbalah Centre may be pricing itself out of the market, while FLG remains essentially free.

Another movement that suggests itself as a CCRM is early Christianity. Paul the Apostle had a new vision on the road to Damascus. This experience brought about his conversion to the budding Jesus movement, upon which he had a dramatic impact. Paul was the driving force in converting gentiles to the "good news." Because of Paul's influence, gentiles were not required to meet the demands of Jewish religious law (i.e., Jewish Culture), just the new faith in Jesus and a primary principle—love. Roman roads and the Greek language facilitated the spread of the new faith throughout the Roman Empire, and, tradition suggests, all the way to Southern India by the end of the first century. Yet Christianity remained a minority religion for 300 years. A new steady state for the entire movement was not established until Constantine converted and established Christianity as the official religion of the Empire. Nevertheless, individuals and some communities met Wallace's "steady state" definition. They would have to for the movement to go on past the first generation.

With the above concerns in mind, the next section is a list of characteristics of the substantive theory that arose out of this study of FLG and to a lesser degree of the Kabbalah center. This list is suggestive for developing a grand theory for CCRMs.

## SUGGESTIONS FOR FURTHER STUDY

1. CCRMs will resurrect past mazeway elements, combined to form a new mazeway—a more satisfying culture.
2. CCRMs will be triggered in part by societal stress (such as modernization, secularization or deprivation).
3. CCRMs will promote volunteerism, increasing the individual's sense of self-worth and connection to the new community.
4. CCRMs will be cross-cultural, appealing mostly to individuals from the originating culture, but they may also appeal to individuals from a host culture who have become dissatisfied with the local mazeway.
5. CCRMs will not stress race/ethnicity, which will make the movement more appealing to those seeking a new mazeway, and which will provide the moral high ground from which to appeal to governmental and legal bodies for protection and justice.
6. CCRMs will have a central, authoritative, charismatic leader. Hence, the extent to which a host culture may influence core CCRM beliefs will be limited by the extent to which the leader is willing to interact with it and the extent to which the leader maintains control.
7. CCRMs will be eclectic, using ancient and modern methods of communication and education. This eclectic approach will allow for broader participation among the members and will provide a broader base for resisting attack.
8. CCRMs will establish non-formal schools to socialize children into the movement.
9. CCRMs will tend to exhibit synergy among its members to produce something greater than the sum of the parts. The results of these interactive forces may be either creative or destructive in the pursuit of a more satisfying culture.
10. CCRMs will include spiritual/altered state of consciousness practices, intrinsic to the new worldview.
11. CCRMs will address health concerns.

12. CCRMs will develop an extensive and varied network from the local to the larger community.


## EDUCATION AND CCRMS

At the outset of this study a central question was asked, along with five supporting questions. I believe the answers have been found.

How does the FLG educate/socialize its members into the FLG community? And what does this tell us about the nature of FLG as a social movement? FLG methodology is about sharing. Techniques are numerous and can shift with cultural and technological preferences. Further, sharing does not include pressure of any kind—except when protesting against human rights abuses. The extent to which one participates is completely self-determined.

Why are people attracted to FLG? FLG gets people's attention. FLG offers the possibility of satisfying felt needs (participation, sharing, improved health, a moral anchor, cultural roots, hope).

How does FLG satisfy needs/reasons for conversion? Conversion is not demanding. The speed and depth of transition is self-determined without pressure or cost. FLG also provides opportunities for creative participation, a sharing community, improved health, achievable and satisfying moral goals, a new vision of hope.

How does the FLG form a new cultural community? The new community is glocal (local and global). Practitioners meet regularly in nearby parks or homes. The local community networks in a number of ways to connect with the larger regional, national and world FLG community. This basic structure allows for the formation of a new cross-cultural community that crosses traditional boundaries, provides a new mazeway, vision, morals, and actual political power.

How does the FLG recruit/instruct followers? The approach of the community is not demanding but supportive. Instruction is generally informal. Small groups meet locally in public parks or private homes to discuss the central text, tell stories, share experiences, and watch videos. Many other sources of instruction and sharing are provided via Internet sites. Further, the community provides the non-formal Ming Hui School for practitioners' children.

How are different educational methods used and why? FLG exhibits a number of traditional and modern methods. Traditional methods include transmission, memorization, question and answer, and meditation. Other methods are more contemporary, seemingly following multiple intelligences theory and metacognitive theory. Why FLG has woven these methods into its own approach was not stated, but the combination appears intuitive.

What are the various forms these methods take? Transmission means accepting truths handed down from the past or from Master Li. The more central the truth, the more likely it is to be memorized. Metacognition is a technique used in the Ming Hui School at the end of each lesson, covering a checklist of behaviors based on truthfulness, compassion and tolerance. Meditation is a series of stylized exercises in which the practitioner applies the principle of truthfulness, compassion and tolerance to his conscious thoughts.

What is communicated through these methods? Every thought and every action must be measured against the central principle—truthfulness, compassion and tolerance.

How are these methods perceived? As neither the members nor the materials reviewed made any attempt to analyze the methods, it is difficult to state unequivocally what the perception of the methods is. What is clear is that they unite past and present methods into a unique FLG approach. The central perception is one clear standard—truthfulness, compassion and tolerance.

How does education promote a new steady state? A new steady state is easier to achieve when there is one authority, one text, all pointing to one principle that cuts across the entire curriculum. Clear standards aid in setting, achieving, and evaluating goals.

## WHAT EDUCATORS CAN LEARN

Regardless of the educational context, educators should find CCRMs of interest because of how they generate passion and solutions. What takes place with adults—sharing and meditation—also takes place in the Ming Hui School. However, the Ming Hui School provides more structure than what takes place FLG adult socialization. In the Ming Hui School, not only is Falun Gong to be learned, but also history, culture and language. With adults, however, Falun Gong is to be learned.

Despite the fact that the Ming Hui School has more direct teaching and more content to be mastered, the malaise that often plagues learners (indeed even teachers) in other institutions does not seem to be a problem in the Ming Hui School. Nor does it appear to be a problem in any of the other non-formal and informal FLG learning environments. Perhaps educators of all sorts will find a number of FLG approaches to education invigorating.

Many of the technical solutions found in FLG are already being used in education—such as the Internet. Yet FLG does not stop at using the Internet to mine information or develop a webpage. FLG develops networks and then connects the networks. FLG provides free software to bust through walls that prevent its learners from having full access. Educators need to reevaluate the extent to which they use their tools and resources and the extent to which their practices liberate and motivate learners.

Similarly, in American public schools, parents are encouraged to volunteer and share. However, in FLG, volunteerism is not limited to making photocopies for the professional teacher, and sharing is not limited to career day. Everyone is welcome to contribute as much as they are able. This practice not only multiplies the teaching force while exponentially reducing costs, it also reconnects learning to the local community and connects communities that were never before connected.

In the West (as in many other parts of the world), education has largely abandoned a connection to ancient texts and ways of knowing in favor of more recent paradigms. FLG has connected ancient and modern, a strategy with which many adherents seem to be a satisfied.

In Western schools, the idea of multiple intelligences has begun to take root (in the Far East, rarely), but it is standard in every Ming Hui School lesson. In the same way, metacognition is just beginning to make inroads into curriculum planning, but in the Ming Hui School, self-evaluation is standard after every lesson. Indeed, self-evaluation in regard to truthfulness, compassion and tolerance is a daily part of every practitioner's life.

An even more radical approach is the use of altered states of consciousness (ASC) through meditation. The extent to which the use of ASC in education might aid in memorization, creativity, metacognition, emotional stability and general good health remains largely untapped in the west, and largely so elsewhere.

FLG motivates others through its moral imperative, which seems self-evident—truthfulness, compassion and tolerance. Applied to the self, to the group, to local society, to the environment and to global society, the general course of action is clear to both children and adults.

In a secularized society, the religious nature of teaching and learning in CCRMs may be off-putting, and the commitment to one leader may be considered dangerous. Yet the speed with which FLG has spread and developed should be cause for reevaluation of one's entire approach to education. In American public education, there is no central text and no charismatic prophet. Perhaps this is as it should be.

What can be adopted is community-based learning that is intensely committed to volunteerism, sharing, networking, multiple intelligences, metacognition, and ASC. As these approaches begin to take root, perhaps a core belief will also emerge. I would not be surprised it if did, and if it resembled truthfulness, compassion and tolerance.

## PRINCIPLES OF EDUCATIONAL EVALUATION

What FLG exhibits throughout the conversion and growth process is a clear principle of evaluation—truth, compassion and tolerance. This principle is easily understandable and easily accepted, regardless of the prospective follower's background. The power of this evaluative principle lies in its universality. It can be universally accepted, universally applied, and it produces a feeling of satisfaction in the student. This satisfaction produces more motivation bringing about more success.

What can educators take away from this study? When success of the student hinges on motivation, it behooves the educator to find ways to motivate the student in the most natural way and to find the hindrances to motivation, the hindrances to satisfaction with the educational culture. As trust in the system is always important for the student to be comfortable with mastering the content, it behooves the educator and the educational system to instill trust.

For trust to be established, a feeling of legitimate authority must also be established. The student needs to feel that what he is learning is correct, authoritative, coming from an authoritative source. He also needs to feel that the method of learning the content is also the authoritative way to learn it. Lack of assurance in the authority of the content and the method undermines the entire learning enterprise. The student may feel that the material is miscellany, untrustworthy and useless.

The power of a FLG education is that there is one principle pervading all elements of the education—that is truth, compassion and tolerance. Regardless of whether the content is mathematics, Chinese language, culture, metacognition or meditation, everything boils down to truth, compassion and tolerance. If something is true, compassionate and tolerant, it is seen as trustworthy.

## EDUCATIONAL IMPERATIVE

In the present American educational system, and many other educational systems in the world, there is no single principle that acts as a benchmark for everything, an absolute standard against which everything can be measured. If educators can find an absolute standard that always works, then they will have found something that the student can always use, can always trust and be satisfied with. They will have solved a major motivational issue in education.

This issue cannot simply be dismissed by pointing out that the practitioner's allegiance is to Li Hongzhi and that a pluralistic society, such as the United States, cannot place ultimate authority in one person with godlike status. To thus dismiss the problem is to condemn many to mediocrity and hopelessness. Indeed, totalitarian societies face the same problem.

## SUMMARY OF CHAPTER 8

What is instructive about revitalization movement theory (including CCRMs) is that one way or another, humans will have connection to the past, spirituality and hope for the future. The extent to which any given revitalization movement forces dramatic conflict depends largely on the extent to which the host society is able to accommodate its critiques. Such critiques will be based upon a vibrant connection to the past, a living spiritual tradition and a faith that the existing structures offer hope for the future.

*Appendix A*

# Informed Consent Form (English)

Consent Form

Participant's name: _______________________________________________

I authorize <u>G. David Rath</u> of the <u>Intercultural Education Department</u>, Biola University, La Mirada, California, and/or any designated research assistants to gather information from me on the topic of how converts are socialized into the practice of Falun Gong.

I understand that the general purpose of the research is to learn how education takes place in the Falun Gong and that the approximate total time of my involvement will be two hours.

I am aware that my participation is voluntary and that I may refuse to participate or discontinue my participation at any time without penalty or loss of benefits to which I am otherwise entitled.

I understand that if, after my participation, I experience any undue anxiety or stress that may have been provoked by the experience or if I have questions about the research or my rights as a participant, <u>G. David Rath</u> will be available for consultation and to provide direction regarding remedial resources in case of questions or problems regarding the research.

The researcher will keep my identity confidential. Personally identifying information will not be released without my written consent.

The potential benefits of the study are the disclosure of the findings of this research to the participant and to society at large.

___________________________________        _______________
Signature                                                                    Date

There are two copies of this consent form included. Please sign one and return it to the researcher with your responses. The other copy you may keep for your records.

Questions and comments may be addressed to <u>G. David Rath</u>, <u>Intercultural Education Department</u>, Biola University, 13800 Biola Ave., La Mirada, CA 90639-0001. Phone: (562) 903-6000.

*Appendix B*

# Informed Consent Form (Chinese)

同意书

参与者姓名: ______________________________________________

本人授权加州La Mirada市, 百欧拉大学 (BIOLA University)跨文化教育
部门的G. David Rath及其研究助理，向我收集有关法轮功修煉者是如何
进入法轮功修煉的相关资料。

我明白此研究的基本目的在瞭解法轮功如何教導學員，而我所参与的时
间约为两小时。

我明白我的参与是自愿的，而我有权在任何时候拒绝参与或中止我的
参与，并且不會受到任何的惩罚或失去任何可享之受益權。

我明白若参加此研究后，如我有產生任何的焦虑、压力，或对此研究及
我作为一个参与者的权益有任何疑问可向G. David Rath作咨询。

研究人员将对个人身份保密. 未经本人书面同意,不得公开任何能辨識本
人的资料. 此研究的潜在受益是研究结果會告知予参與者及一般社会大
众.

签名______________________________        日期__________________

此同意书共有两份。请把其中签好的一份及问券交回，並請自行保留
另一份以作参考.

若有任何的疑问或意见，请联系<u>G. David Rath</u>, <u>Intercultural Education Department</u>, Biola University, 13800 Biola Ave., La Mirada, CA 90639-0001. Phone: (562) 903-6000.

*Appendix C*

# Questionnaire

Questionnaire (问券调查)          Code # (编号): _______________

1. Your age is (您的年龄是):
□ 18-30          □ 50-60
□ 30-40          □ 60-70
□ 40-50          □ 70+

2. Highest Education Level  (教育程度):
□ Junior High Graduate (初中毕业)
□ High School Graduate (高中毕业)
□ Technical School (专科), Specialization (主修): ____________________
□ Bachelor's Degree (学士学位), Specialization (主修): ________________
□ Master's Degree (硕士学位), Specialization (主修):_________________
□ Doctoral Degree (博士学位), Specialization (主修):_________________

3. Marital Status (婚姻状况):
□ Single (单身)          □ Married (结婚)          □ Divorced (离婚)
□ Separated (分居)       □ Widowed (守寡)

4. Do you have any children? (您有任何孩子吗)?          □ Yes          □ No
   Grandchildren? (孙子/孙女)                          □ Yes          □ No

## *Appendix D*

# Phase One Interview Guide For Practitioners

1. Tell me how you became involved with the Falun Gong.

   请告诉我您是如何开始修煉法轮功?

2. Tell me what it has been like to be involved with the Falun Gong.

   请告诉我您觉得修煉法轮功的感觉如何?

3 Why do you stay with the Falun Gong if it is so hated/persecuted?

   为什么法轮功遭受迫害您仍要继续修煉法轮功?

4. How has this interview been for you?

   您觉得这访谈如何?

# Phase Two Interview Guide For Practitioners

1. How did you first hear about "truth, compassion, and tolerance?
   您是如何第一次聽到 "真, 善, 忍"?

2. Tell me about the FLG groups you meet with and why?
   您怎樣跟其他的法輪功學員碰面或聚會? 那聚會的原因呢?

3. Have you ever had any supernormal experiences in practicing FLG? (visions, healing, 3rd eye, levels/dimensions)?

   您修煉法輪功有經歷過任何的特異功能現象嗎?
   (異象, 醫治, 第三眼(天眼通), 層次)?

4. What kind of support do you get in FLG? Any pressure?
   在法輪功裡, 您得什麼支持? 有任何的壓力嗎?

5. Is there anything about FLG that an observer/researcher is likely to miss?
   法輪功的哪些方面是一個觀察員或者研究員會容易錯過的?

6. How do you learn / help others to reach a new level of practice?
   您如何學習或幫助其他學員達到新的層次?

7. What is the highest level you have reached? How did you reach it?
   您的最高層次是哪一級呢? 您是如何達到呢?

8. What are your goals? (Of these, which is most important to you?)
   您的目標有那些? (那個目標對您來說是最重要的?)

9. How has this interview been for you?
   您覺得這訪談如何?

*Appendix F*

# Interview Guide For The Principal

1.  Please tell me about the Ming Hui School.

    麻煩您給我講有關明慧學校的情況吧.

2.  What subjects are taught?

    學校教授的科目有那哪些?

3.  In what ways is the Ming Hui school special, distinct from other schools (i.e. Cram Schools, public school)?

    明慧學校跟一般(的公立)學校和以補習為主的輔導學校有什麼區別? 明慧學校的特點在哪裡? (不同或特別的地方有哪些)?

4.  What are the goals of the school and how are they achieved?

    學校的目標是什麼? (這些目標是怎麼實現的?)

5.  What benefits do students experience because of the Ming Hui school?

    您的孩子在明慧學校有哪些特別的收獲呢?

6.  How do you assess student learning?

    你們如何來評估學生的學習情況呢?

7.  How has this interview been for you?

    您覺得這訪談如何?

*Appendix G*

# Interview Guide For Parents

1. How did you decide to send your child to the Ming Hui school?

   您是如何決定送您的小孩到明慧學校上學的?

2. What subjects does your child study here?

   您的小孩在這裡學習哪些科目?

3. In what ways is the Ming Hui school special, distinct from other schools (i.e. Cram Schools, public school)?

   明慧學校跟一般般(的公立)學校和以補習為主的輔導學校有什麼區別? 明慧學校的特點在哪裡?

4. What benefits have you or your child experienced because of the Ming Hui school?

   您和您的孩子在明慧學校有哪些特別的收獲呢?

5. How has this interview been for you?

   您覺得這訪談如何?

# References

*9-Day lecture video.* (2007). Retrieved April 18, 2008, from http://www.falundafa .org/ bul/audio-video/audiovideo_9video.html

Aberle, D. F. (1960). A note on relative deprivation as applied to millenarian and other cult movements. In S. Thrupp (Ed.), *Millenial dreams in action: Essays in comparative study* (pp. 209-224). The Hague: Mouton & Co.

—— (1982). *The Peyote religion among the Navaho* (2 ed.). Chicago: Unviersity of Chicago Press.

*About the early morning exercises program on Minghui radio (Updated).* (2008). Retrieved April 19, 2008, from http://www.clearwisdom.net/emh/ articles/2008/1/10/93147.html

*About us.* (2008). Retrieved May 5, 2008, from http://sfk.org/en/about/staff

*Additional persecution news from China - March 5, 2008 (42 Reports).* (2008). Retrieved March 5, 2008, from http://www.clearwisdom.net/emh/articles/ 2008/3/18/95464.html

Algar, H. (2002). *Wahhabism: A critical essay.* Oneonta, New York: Islamic Publications International.

Andrade, A. (1999). *My Falun Dafa experiences.* Retrieved April, 19, 2008, from http://www.umich.edu/~falun/Experience/Augusto_eng.html

Aristotle. (2002). Nicomachean ethics. In R. Crisp (Ed.), *Cambridge texts in the history of philosophy.* Cambridge, MA: Cambridge Univesity Press.

Atkinson, R., & Flint, J. (2004). Snowball sampling. In M. S. Lewis-Beck, A. Bryman & T. F. Liao (Eds.), *The SAGE encyclopedia of social science research methods* (Vol. 3, pp. 1043-1044). Thousand Oaks, CA: SAGE Publications.

*Audio & video materials.* (2007). Retrieved April 18, 2008, from http://www. falundafa.org/bul/audio-video/audiovideo_9video.html)

*Awards & media reports to master (Selected Photos).* (2008). Retrieved March 9, 2008, from http://photo.minghui.org/images/u_master/E_awards_and_media _reports_master_300_1.htm

Barnes, A. (2006). *Kabbalah: is Madonna losing her religion?* Retrieved May 5, 2008, from http://www.independent.co.uk/news/uk/this-britain/kabbalah-is-madonna-losing-her-religion-407250.html

Beckford, J. A. (2000). "Start together and finish together": Shifts in the premises and paradigms underlying the scientific study of religion. *Journal for the Scientific Study of Religion, 39*(4), 481-495.

—— (2004). New religious movements and globalization. In P. C. Lucas & T. Robbins (Eds.), *New religious movements in the 21st century: Legal, political, and social challenges in global perspective* (pp. 253-263). New York: Routledge.

*Belgium: Enthusiastic reception for the Chinese spectacular.* (2008). Retrieved April 23, 2008, from http://www.clearharmony.net/articles/200803/43661.html

Bell, M. R., & Boas, T. C. (2003). Falun Gong and the internet: Evangelism, community, and struggle for survival. *Nova Religio: The Journal of Alternative and Emergent Religions, 6*(2), 277-293

Berg, K. (2005). *God wears lipstick: Kabbalah for women.* Los Angeles: Kabbalah Centre International.

Berg, Y. (2004). *The power of Kabbalah: Technology for the woul* (4 ed.). New York: Kabbalah Publishing.

Berg, Y. (2008). *Red string DVD.* Los Angeles: Kabbalah Publishing.

Berthelsen, C. (2008). O.C. official 'insulted' by China letter; Supervisors' chairman Norby is asked not to recognize upcoming events backed by Falun Gong supporters [Electronic Version]. *Los Angeles Times*, Part B; P. 3,

Bright, B. (1993). *Have you heard of the four spiritual laws?* Peachtree City, GA: New Life Publications.

*Brisbane audience's spectacular finale reactions.* (2008). Retrieved April 23, 2008, from http://english.ntdtv.com/?c=256&a=2692

Bromley, D. G. (1998). New religious movements. *Encyclopedia of Religion and Society.* Retrieved January 11, 2008, from http://hirr.hartsem.edu/ency /NRM.htm

Bryant, A., & Charmaz, K. (Eds.). (2007). *The SAGE handbook of grounded theory.* Thousand Oaks, CA: Sage Publications, Ltd.

Burgdoff, C. A. (2003). How Falun Gong practice undermines Li Hongzhi's totalistic rhetoric. *Nova Religio: The Journal of Alternative and Emergent Religions, 6*(2), 332–347.

Burke, E. (2001). *Reflections on the revolution in France* (Vol. 24, Part 3). New York: P.F. Collier & Son, 1909–14; Bartleby.com.

*Business Phone and Fax Numbers.* (n.d.). Retrieved April 19, 2008, from http:// www. clarifythetruthinchina.com/index.php?article_file=biz.html

Byrne, T. (2008). From acrobats to pageantry, celebrating Chinese culture [Electronic Version]. *The Boston Globe.* Retrieved April 25, 2008, from http://www.boston.com/ae/theater_arts/articles/2008/01/11/from_acrobats_to_pageantry_celebrating_chinese_culture/

Caiju & Huang, K. (2007). New York: 5000-Person parade held on broadway to clarify the truth (Photos). Retrieved Apirl 22, 2008, from http://www. clearwisdom. net/emh/articles/2007/4/10/84418.html

Carter, L. F. (1990). *Charisma and control in Rajneeshpuram: The role of shared values in the creation of a community*. Cambridge, MA: Cambridge University Press.

Chan, C. S.-c. (2004). The Falun Gong in China: A sociological perspective. *The China Quarterly*, 665-683.

China plans jam-proof communications satellite to keep ahead of Falungong. (2004). Retrieved April 20, 2008, from http://www.cesnur.org/2004/falun_ 001.htm

*Chronicle of major events of Falun Dafa (3rd Edition)*. (2004, March 15, 2004). Retrieved March 9, 2008, from http://www.pureinsight.org/pi/index. php?news=2097

Clearwisdom.net. (2004). *New software - Ultrasurf 6.2 - set to break internet blockade*. Retrieved July 15, 2007, from http://www.clearwisdom. net/emh/articles/ 2004/8/25/51717.html

*Community programs*. (2006). Retrieved April 24, 2008, from http://www.kabbalah .com/programs.html

*Complete reference to China/Chinese newspapers, news services, and news portal sites*. (2008). Retrieved April 19, 2008, from http://chinasite.com/Media/ Newspaper.html

Corbin, J. M., & Strauss, A. (1990). Grounded Theory Research: Procedures, Canons, and Evaluative Criteria. *Qualitative Sociology, 13*(1), 3-21.

Creswell, J. W. (1998). *Qualitative inquiry and research design: Choosing among five traditions*. Thousand Oaks, CA: Sage.

—— (2003). *Research design: Qualitative, quantitative, and mixed methods approaches* (2nd ed.). Thousand Oaks, CA: Sage.

Cui, L. (1989a, April 20-24). Fitness and health through Qigong. *Beijing Review, 32*, 20-24.

—— (1989b, April 20-24). Qigong on Qinghua campus. *Beijing Review, 32*, 24-26.

Culp, L. K. (Ed.). (1999). *Falun Gong stories: A journey to enlightenment*. Buford, GA: Golden Lotus Press.

*Cult* [Electronic Version]. (2000). *The American Heritage® Dictionary of the English Language*. Retrieved June 17, 2008, from http://www.bartleby.com/61/97/ C0799700.html

*Cultivating well and following the path of assisting master in Fa Rectification*. (2008). Retrieved April 19, 2008, from http://www.clearwisdom.net/emh/articles /2008/3/20/95538.html

*Curriculum*. (2008). Retrieved April 24, 2008, from http://sfk.org/en/curriculum

Dawson, L. (2002). Crisis of charasmatic legitimacy and violent behavior. In D. G. Bromley & J. G. Melton (Eds.), *Cults, Religion, and Violence* (pp. 80-101). Cambridge: Cambridge University Press.

Dawson, L. L. (1998). The cultural significance of new religious movements and globalization: A theoretical prolegomenon. *Journal for the Scientific Study of Religion, 37*(4), 580-595.

—— (2001). The cultural significance of new religious movements: The case of Soka Gakkai. *Association for the Sociology of Religion, 62*(3), 337-364.

—— (2003). *Cults and new religious movements: A reader*. Malden, MA: Blackwell Publishing.

deMarrais, K. B., & Lapan, S. D. (Eds.). (2004). *Foundations for research: Methods of inquiry in education and the social sciences*. Mahwah, NJ: Lawrence Erlbaum Associates.

Dillow, G. (2008). Chinese letter not letter perfect [Electronic Version]. *Orange County Register*. Retrieved May 1, 2008, from http://www.ocregister.com/ column/ Chinese-letter-government-1956188-officials-norby

Dubuisson, D. (2003). *The Western construction of religion: Myths, knowledge, and ideology* (W. Sayers, Trans.). Baltimore, MD: Johns Hopkins University Press.

Els, H. (1990). 'Inkatha Yenkululeko Yesizwe' as cultural revitalization movement. *South African Journal of Ethnology, 13*, 77-88.

*Exercise music*. (n.d.). Retrieved April 19, 2008, from http://www.falundafa.org /bul/ audio-video/audiovideo.html

*Exercises of Falun Dafa*. (n.d.). Retrieved April 19, 2008, from www.falundafa.org. nz/excerices.htm

Fahey, R. (2007, February 8, 2007). New Year inspires glittering spectacle. *The Boston Globe,* p. Reg. 7,

*Falun Dafa (Falun Gong) Classes*. (2008a). Retrieved April 19, 2008, from http: //www.its.caltech.edu/~falun/9dayseminar.html

*Falun Dafa: Practice sites in Los Angeles area & Santa Barbara*. (2008b). Retrieved April 18, 2008, from http://www.its.caltech.edu/~falun/LA_practice.html

*Falun Gong holds grand parade in Los Angeles [Electronic Version]*. (2008). Retrieved April 22, 2008, from http://en.epochtimes.com/news/8-2-24/66565.html

Feng, A. Y. (May 14, 2001). *My understanding of Fa-Rectification - Part 1*. Retrieved April 19, 2008, from http://www.pureinsight.org/pi/print_version. php?id=662

Feng, C. (2008). *Text messaging increasingly popular to promote quitting the CCP*. Retrieved April 19, 2008, from http://en.epochtimes.com/news/8-1-19/64311. html

Fenn, R. K. (1972). Toward a new sociology of religion. *Journal for the Scientific Study of Religion, 11*(1), 16-32.

Flavell, J. H. (1979). Metacognition and cognitive monitoring: A new area of cognitive-developmental inquiry. *American Psychologist, 34*(10), 906-911.

Fontana, A., & Frey, J. H. (1994). Interviewing: The art of science. In N. K. Denzin & Y. Lincoln (Eds.), *Handbook of qualitative research* (pp. 361-376). Thousand Oaks, CA: Sage.

*Free downloads for learning Falun Dafa*. (2002). Retrieved April 19, 2008, from www.falunau.org/practicedownloads.htm

Gardner, H. (1999). *Intelligence reframed: Multiple intelligences for the 21st century*. New York: Basic Books.

*Germany: European Divine Land marching band gives its first performance at a multicultural festival in Hamburg (Photos)*. (2007). Retrieved April 22, 2008, from http://truthinchina.wordpress.com/2007/09/29/germany-european-divine-land-marching-band-gives-its-first-performance-at-a-multicultural-festival-in-hamburg-photos/

Glaser, B. G. (1978). *Theoretical sensitivity: Advances in the methodology of Grounded Theory*. Mill Valley, CA: Sociology Press.

Glaser, B. G., & Strauss, A. L. (2006). *The discovery of Grounded Theory: Strategies for qualitative research*. New Brunswick, Canada: Aldine Traction.

Glock, C. Y. (1964). The role of deprivation in the origin and evolution of religious groups. In R. Lee & M. E. Marty (Eds.), *Religion and social conflict* (pp. 24-36). New York: Oxford University Press.

*Glossary.* (n.d.). Retrieved April 19, 2008, from http://www.clearwisdom.net/emh/glossary.html

Goldberg, A. B., & Thomson, K. (2005). *What's behind Hollywood's fascination with Kabbalah?* Retrieved May 5, 2008, from http://abcnews.go.com/ print?id=855125

*Gruesome death toll - 3158 confirmed dead, tens of thousands more unconfirmed.* (May 28, 2008). Retrieved May 29, 2008, from http://www.clearwisdom.net/emh/special_column/death_cases/death_list.html

Gurney, J. N., & Tierney, K. J. (1982). Relative deprivation and social movements. *The Sociological Quarterly, 23*(Winter), 33-47.

Haithman, D. (2008). Art or politics? Ties to spiritual sect cast shadow on Chinese New Year Spectacular. *Los Angeles Times,* pp. Part E, 1,

Hak, D. H. (1998). Deprivation theory. *Encyclopedia of Religion and Society.* Retrieved January 11, 2008, from http://hirr.hartsem.edu/ency/deprivation. htm

Hannigan, J. A. (1991). Social movement theory and the sociology of religion. *Sociological Analysis, 52,* 311-331.

Harkin, M. E. (Ed.). (2004). *Reassessing revitalization movements: Perspectives from North America and the Pacific Islands*. Lincoln: University of Nebraska Press.

Hexham, I., & Poewe, K. (1998). *New religions as global cultures*. Boulder, CO: Westview.

Hinnells, J. R. (2005). *The Routledge companion to the study of religion*. New York: Routledge.

*How to make the best use of the "Irina Phone Script."* (n.d.). Retrieved April 19, 2008, from http://www.clarifythetruthinchina.com/index.php?article_file=call-scripts/bestuseof.html

Hsu, E. (2001). *Innovation in Chinese medicine*. New York: Cambridge University Press.

Hua, V. (2006). Falun Gong dispute hangs over S.F. Chinese parade. Retrieved April 22, 2008, from http://www.sfgate.com/cgi-bin/article.cgi?file=/ c/a/2006/01/30/MNGO7GVLJK1.DTL

Huang, K., & Ying, W. (2008). *Western USA Fa conference held in Los Angeles, practitioners share their cultivation experiences (Photos).* Retrieved April 22, 2008, from http://www.clearwisdom.net/emh/articles/2008/2/26/ 94812.html

Human Rights Watch Report. (2002). *Dangerous meditation: China's campaign against Falun Gong* (Vol. 8-9). New York: Author.

Irons, E. (2003). Falun Gong and the sectarian religion paradigm. *Nova Religio: The Journal of Alternative and Emergent Religions, 6*(2), 244-262.

Jackson, J. B. (2004). Recontextualizing revitalization: Cosmology and cultural stability in the adoption of Peyotism among the Yuchi. In M. E. Harkin (Ed.), *Reassessing revitalization movements: Perspectives from North America and the Pacific Islands* (pp. 183-205). Lincoln: University of Nebraska Press.

Jing, X. (2007). *Minnesota: Mid-USA Falun Dafa Experience Sharing Conference held in Minneapolis - revered Master sends message of congratulations and encouragement (Photos)*. Retrieved April 22, 2008, from http://www. clearwisdom. net/emh/articles/2007/9/23/89860.html

*KCP Direction*. (2008). Retrieved April 30, 2008, from http://www.youtube.com/ watch?v=YIWP-cKa7Wg&eurl=http://sfk.org/en/kcp

Kent, A. (2006). *Divinity and diversity: A Hindu revitalization movement in Malaysia*. Honolulu: University of Hawaii Press.

Klass, M. (1995). *Ordered universes: Approaches to the anthropology of religion*. Boulder, CO: Westview Press.

*Kong Rong*. (2003). *Ming Hui school lesson plan: (1) Kong Rong offering pears*. Retrieved April 30, 2008, from http://www.pureinsight.org/pi/index.php ?news=1871

Krishan, Y. (1997). *The doctrine of Karma: Its origin and development in Brāhmaṇical, Buddhist, and Jaina traditions*. Delhi, India: Motilal Banarsidass.

Kuo, E. C. Y. (1992). *Confucianism as political discourse in Singapore: The case of an incomplete revitalization movement*. Singapore, Malaysia: National University of Singapore.

Kushner, G. (1965). An African revitalization movement: Mau Mau. *Anthropos, 60*(1), 763-802.

Lai, H. H. (2003). The religious revival in China. *Copenhagen Journal of Asian Studies, 18*, 40-64.

Lam, K.-C. (2004). *Tai Chi for staying young: The gentle way to health and well-being*. New York: Fireside

*Law of Cause and Effect: Authors of Pornographic Books Met Karmic Retribution*. (2005). Retrieved April 20, 2008, from http://www.pureinsight.org/pi/ index. php?news=3258

*Learn simple Chinese phrases!* (n.d.). Retrieved April 19, 2008, from http://www. clarifythetruthinchina.com/index.php?article_file=learn.html

*Learning Falun Dafa*. (2008). Retrieved April 19, 2008, from http://www.stanford. edu/group/falun/eng/start.htm

Leung, B. (2002). China and Falun Gong: Party and society relations in the modern era. *Journal of Contemporary China, 11*(33), 761–784.

Li, H. (2000). *Falun Dafa: Essentials for further advancement*. New York: Universe Publications.

—— (2001). *Falun Gong*. Retrieved April 30, 2004, from http://falundafa.org/ eng/ books.htm

—— (2003). *Zhuan Falun*. Retrieved May 12, 2006, from http://falundafa.org /eng/ books.htm

—— (2007). *Teacher's collected articles and lectures: 2003 and 2004*. Retrieved April 24, 2008, from http://falundafa.org/book/eng/pdf/collected2003-2004.pdf

—— (2008). *Clarification*. Retrieved April 19, 2008, from http://www.pureinsight. org/pi/index.php?news=5318

Li, J. (2006). *How did Falun Gong become a political movement?* Paper presented at the American Sociological Association. Retrieved June 13, 2008, from http:// www.allacademic.com/meta/p102593_index.html

—— (2007). *The Divine Performing Arts Troupe will reach 650,000 in its 2008 global tour*. Retrieved April 22, 2008, from http://www.bestchineseshows. com/node/3504

Lifton, R. J. (2000). *Destroying the world to save it: Aum Shinrikyo, apocalyptic violence, and the new global terrorism*. New York: Holt Paperbacks.

Lindholm, C. (1992). Charisma, crowd psychology and altered states of consciousness. *Culture, Medicine and Psychiatry, 16*(3), 287-310.

Linton, R. (1943). Nativistic movements. *American Anthropologist, 45*(2), 230-240.

Little, M. (2008). Ontario's Education Minister says the Chinese spectacular Is 'wonderful'. Retrieved April 23, 2008, from http://chinaview.wordpress .com/2008/01/20/ontarios-education-minister-says-the-chinese-spectacular-is-wonderful/

Livesey, C. (2008, April 14, 2008). *Overt participant observation*. Retrieved June 19, 2008, from http://www.sociology.org.uk/methpo7.htm

*Los Angeles, California: Candlelight vigil held in front of Chinese Embassy to commemorate practitioners tortured to death in China (Photos)*. (2008). Retrieved April 22, 2008, from http://www.clearwisdom.net/emh/articles /2008/2/24/94738.html

Lowe, S. (2003). Chinese and international contexts for the rise of Falun Gong. *Nova Religio: The Journal of Alternative and Emergent Religions, 6*(2), 263-276.

Lu, Y. (2005). Entrepreneurial logistics and the evolution of Falun Gong [Electronic Version]. *Journal for the Scientific Study of Religion*, 173-185,

Lucas, P. C. (2004). The future of new and minority religions in the twenty-first century: Religious freedom under global siege. In P. C. Lucas & T. Robbins (Eds.), *New religious movements in the twenty-first century: Legal, political, and social challenges in global perspective* (pp. 341-357). New York: Routledge.

Luona, & Xinyu. (2007). *Australia: Falun Dafa practitioner wins lawsuit against Bo Xilai*. Retrieved April 20, 2008, from http://truthinchina.wordpress.com/2007/11/09/australia-falun-dafa-practitioner-wins-lawsuit-against-bo-xilai

Luscombe, B. (2006). *Exclusive: Madonna speaks about her "Big, Big Project."* Retrieved May 5, 2008, from http://www.time.com/time/world/article /0,8599,1222449,00.html

Madonna & Fulvimari, J. (2003). *The English roses*. New York: Callaway.

Madonna & Long, L. (2003). *Mr. Peabody's apples*. New York: Callaway.

Madonna & Spirin, G. (2004). *Yakov and the seven thieves*. New York: Callaway.

Maestas N., & Gaillot, S. (2008a). *Evaluating the Spirituality for Kids After-School Program [Electronic Version]*. Retrieved May 1, 2008, from http:// rand.org/pubs/technical_reports/2008/RAND_TR575.sum.pdf

Maestas, N., & Gaillot, S. (2008b). *An outcome evaluation of the Spirituality for Kids Program [Electronic Version]*. Retrieved May 1, 2008, from http://rand. org/pubs/technical_reports/2008/RAND_TR575.pdf

Malaysia. (2008). *Malaysia cancels dance troupe show at China's request over Falun Gong content*. (2008). Retrieved April 1, 2008, from http://www. iht.com/articles/ap/2008/03/24/news/Malaysia-Canceled-Show.php

Marshall, C. (2006). *A festive parade is politicized over exclusion of Falun Gong*. Retrieved April 22, 2008, from http://www.nytimes.com/2006/02/11/ national/11parade.html?partner=rssnyt&emc=rss

*Mass mailing.* (2002). Retrieved April 19, 2008, from http://www.dit-inc.us/ massemail.php

McLoughlin, W. G. (1978). *Revivals, awakenings, and reform: An essay on religion and social change in America, 1607-1977.* Chicago: University of Chicago Press.

McMullen, A. (2004). Canny about conflict: Nativism, revitalization, and the invention of tradition in native southeastern New England. In M. E. Harkin (Ed.), *Reassessing revitalization movements: Perspectives from north America and the pacific islands* (pp. 261-277). Lincoln: University of Nebraska Press.

Morais, R. C. (2006). *When all else fails: Threats.* Retrieved April 22, 2008, from http://www.forbes.com/2006/02/10/china-falun-gong_0210falungong_ print.html

Moyers, B. (1995). *Healing and the mind.* New York: Main Street Books.

*My experience of clarifying the truth in Vietnam.* (2008). Retrieved April 19, 2008, from http://www.clearwisdom.net/emh/articles/2008/3/2/94965.html

Newberg, A., D'Aquili, E., & Rause, V. (2001). *Why God won't go away: Brain science & the biology of belief.* New York: Ballantine Books.

*News and media > China.* Retrieved April 19, 2008, from http://dir.yahoo.com/ News_and_Media/By_Region/Countries/China/

NTDTV. (2008). *Falun Gong in Chicago 2008 Thanksgiving Parade.* Retrieved April 22, 2008, from http://video.aol.com/video-detail/falun-gong-in-chicago-2008-thanksgiving-parade/1707867244

*Ongoing lectures.* (2004). Retrieved March 4, 2008, from http://www.kabbalah. com/ k/index.php/p=locations/a/21

Ownby, D. (2000). *Falun Gong as a cultural revitalization movement: An historian looks at contemporary China.* Paper presented at the Transnational China Project Commentary, Rice University, Houston, TX.

—— (2003a). The Falun Gong in the new world. *European Journal of East Asian Studies, 2*(2), 303-320.

—— (2003b). A History for Falun Gong: Popular religion and the Chinese state since the Ming Dynasty. *Nova Religio: The Journal of Alternative and Emergent Religions, 6*(2), 223-243.

—— (2007). Qigong, Falun Gong, and the body politic in contemporary China. In L. M. Jensen & T. B. Weston (Eds.), *China's transformations: The stories beyond the headlines* (pp. 90-111). Lanham, Maryland: Rowman & Littlefield Publishers.

Palmer, D. A. (2005). *La fièvre du Qigong: Guérison, religion et politique en Chine, 1949-1999.* Unpublished Recherches d'histoire et de sciences sociales, Ecole des hautes études en sciences sociales, Paris.

Palmer, S. J. (2003). From healing to protest: Conversion patterns among the practitioners of Falun Gong. *Nova Religio: The Journal of Alternative and Emergent Religions, 6*(2), 348-364.

Parker, N. (2004). What is Falun Gong? An introduction to Falun Gong: How it developed in China and around the world [Electronic Version]. *Compassion: A Journal of Falun Dafa Around the World,* 41. Retrieved April 21, 2008, from http://www. faluninfo.net/compassion5/FalunGong Introduction.htm

Penny, B. (2003). The life and times of Li Hongzhi: Falun Gong and religious biography. *The China Quarterly, 175,* 643-661.

*Personal cultivation.* (2008). Retrieved April 22, 2008, from http://www.clear wisdom.net/emh/31/

Pigliucci, M. (2004). God in the brain. *Skeptic, 10*(4), 82-83.

Poole, S. M. (2006). Chinese dissident attacked at home: Cox News Service.

Porter, N. (2003). *Falun Gong in the United States: An ethnographic study.* University of South Florida, Tampa.

——— (2005). Professional practitioners and contact persons explicating special types of Falun Gong practitioners. *Nova Religio: The Journal of Alternative and Emergent Religions, 9*(2), 62-83.

*Practitioners bring traditional Chinese culture to the Hollywood Christmas Parade (Photos).* (2007). Retrieved April 22, 2008, from http://truthinchina. wordpress. com/2007/11/29/practitioners-bring-traditional-chinese-culture-to-the-hollywood-christmas-parade-photos/

*Prison officials and police phone numbers.* (n.d.). Retrieved April 19, 2008, from http://www.clarifythetruthinchina.com/index.php?article_file=prison.html

*Proclamations: A collection of proclamations and resolutions issued in support of the Human Rights Torch Relay.* (2008). Retrieved April 20, 2008, from http://www. humanrightstorch.org/news/proclamations/

*Protesters hold Falun Dafa banner outside Chinese embassy in Kuala Lumpur, Malaysia.* (2008). Retrieved April 21, 2008, from http://www.philly.com/ philly/wires/    ap/news/world/20080420_ap_olympicflamearrivesinmalaysia. html?imageId=7675044

*Refugees: Seeking solutions to a global concern.* (2004). Retrieved April 20, 2008, from http://www.loc.gov/law/find/hearings/pdf/00137802971.pdf

Robbins, T. (1988). *Cults, converts and charisma.* London: Sage.

——— (2000). "Quo Vadis" the scientific study of new religious movements? *Journal for the Scientific Study of Religion, 39*(4), 515-523.

Robbins, T., Anthony, D., & Curtis, T. (1975). Youth culture religious movements. *Sociological Quarterly, 16*(1), 48-64.

Robertson, R. (1992). *Globalization: Social theory and global culture.* London: Sage.

*Rooting out my every thought of lust.* (2008). Retrieved April 20, 2008, from http:// www.pureinsight.org/pi/index.php?news=5296;

Rosett, C. (2002). *Will Chinese repression play in Peoria? Beijing's campaign against an "evil cult" comes to America. [Electronic Version].* Retrieved April 22, 2008, from http://www.opinionjournal.com/columnists/cRosett/ ?id=105001666

Ross, A. V. I. (2006). Cradle, manger, granary: Carving the body from the nation's sacred flesh. *Journal of Religion & Society, 8*, 1-12.

Saliba, J. A. (1996). *Understanding new religious movements.* Grand Rapids, MI: Eerdmans.

Schechter, D. (2001). *Falun Gong's challenge to China: Spiritual practice or "evil cult"?* New York: Akashic Books.

*Script 04.* (n.d.). Retrieved April 19, 2008, from http://www.clarifythetruthin china. com/index.php?article_file=call-scripts/04_en_script.html

Shupe, A. (1991). Globalization versus religious nativism: Japan's Soka Gakkai in the world arena. In R. Robertson & W. R. Garret (Eds.), *Religion and global order*. New York: Paragon House.

Siegel, R. K. (1989). *Intoxication: Life in pursuit of artificial paradise*. New York: Dutton.

Siikala, J. (2004). Priests and prophets: The politics of voice in the Pacific. In M. E. Harkin (Ed.), *Reassessing revitalization movements: Perspectives from North America and the Pacific Islands* (pp. 88-103). Lincoln: University of Nebraska Press.

Slingerland, E. (2003). *Effortless action: Wu-wei as conceptual metaphor and spiritual ideal in early China*. New York: Oxford University Press.

Stark, R. (1997). *The rise of Christianity: How the obscure, marginal Jesus Movement became the dominant religious force in the Western world in a few centuries*. San Francisco: Harper Collins.

Stark, R., & Bainbridge, W. S. (1985). *The future of religion: Secularization, revival and cult formations*. Berkeley: University of California Press.

Stark, R., & Bainbridge, W. S. (1987). *A theory of religion*. New York: Peter Lang.

Stephen, M. (1997). Cargo cults, cultural creativity, and autonomous imagination. *Ethnos, 25*(3), 333-358.

Strauss, A., & Corbin, J. M. (1998). *Basics of qualitative research: Second edition: Techniques and procedures for developing Grounded Theory* (2nd ed.). Thousand Oaks, CA: Sage Publications.

Streubert, H. J., & Carpenter, D. R. (1999). *Qualitative research in nursing: Advancing the humanistic imperative* (2nd ed.). Philadelphia: Lippincott, Williams, & Wilkins.

*Table of lawsuits filed against former Chinese leader Jiang Zemin and his followers by Falun Gong practitioners around the world (from 2001 to August 2004)*. (2004). Retrieved April 20, 2008, from http://www.clearwisdom.net/emh/articles/2004/8/29/51876p.html

*Taiwan Minghui School summer camps receive warm appreciation from all*. (2004). Retrieved April 19, 2008, from http://clearharmony.net/articles/200411/ 22994.html

Tanner, J. C. (2002). *Behind Falun Gong's satellite hack - first mile - cult hijacks satellite signal - brief article*. Retrieved April 20, 2008, from http://find articles.com/p/articles/mi_m0FGI/is_8_13/ai_91204584

Thornton, P. M. (2002). Framing dissent in contemporary China: Irony, ambiguity and metonymy. *The China Quarterly, 171*, 661-681.

Tong, J. (2002). An organizational analysis of the Falun Gong: Structure, communications, rinancing. *The China Quarterly, 171*, 636-660.

*United States: Falun Gong practitioners and other groups in Los Angeles call on U.S. government to bring criminal CCP agents to justice*. (2008). Retrieved April 22, 2008, from http://www.clearharmony.net/articles/200602/31408.html

Waley, A. (1956). *The analectics of Confucius*. London: George Allen & Unwin Ltd.

Walker, S. (2008 ). *(Falun) Gong New Year event mere propaganda: You don't get well, but you do get the point at tacky New Year event*. Retrieved April 23, 2008, from http://www.thestar.com/entertainment/article/295651

Wallace, A. F. C. (1956). Revitalization movements. *American Anthropologist, 58*(2), 264-281.

—— 1966). *Religion: an Anthropological View.* New York: Random House.

—— (2004). Foreward. In M. E. Harkin (Ed.), *Reassessing revitalization movements: Perspectives from North America and the Pacific Islands* (pp. vii-xi). Lincoln: University of Nebraska Press.

Wang, Y. (2008). *San Francisco: Falun Gong contingent impressive in the St. Patrick's Day Parade (Photos).* Retrieved April 22, 2008, from http://www.clear wisdom.net/emh/articles/2008/3/18/95453.html

Warren, K. B. (1998). *Indigenous movements and their critics: Pan-Maya activism in Guatemala.* Princeton, MA: Princeton University Press.

Wen, C. (2007). *An unofficial channel across the Taiwan Straits: How Taiwan's Falun Gong practitioners help their mainland compatriots break through the communist regime's information blockade.* Retrieved February 7, 2008, from http://en. epoch-times.com/news/7-12-29/63377.html

Wessinger, C. (2003). Falun Gong Symposium Introduction and Glossary. *Nova Religio: The Journal of Alternative and Emergent Religions, 6*(2), 215-222.

*What Shanshan saw in other dimensions (I).* (2001). Retrieved May 1, 2008, from http://www.pureinsight.org/pi/index.php?news=307

*What Spirituality For Kids does.* (2008). Retrieved April 24, 2008, from http://sfk. org/en/print/welcome

When art gets political (or not). (2008, April 12). *Canberra Times,* p. 8,

*Whoever plays with fire gets burnt -- Xinhua commentary on FalunGong's TV hijacking.* (2002). Retrieved April 20, 2008, from http://www.china-embassy.org/eng/ zt/ppflg/t36615.htm

Wimberley, D. W. (1989). Religion and role-identity: A structural symbolic interactionist conception of religiosity. *The Sociological Quarterly, 30*(1), 125-142.

Winkelman, M. (1986). Magico-Religious practitioner types and socioeconomic conditions. *Cross-Cultural Research, 20,* 17-46.

—— (1997). Altered states of consciousness and religious behavior. In S. D. Glazier (Ed.), *Anthropology of religion: A handbook* (pp. 393-428). Westport, CT: Greenwood Press.

Yardeni, Y. (2008). Worldwide classroom--Kabbalistic astrology. Retrieved May 5, 2008, from http://tv.kabbalah.com/product_info.php?products_id=612

York, M. (1995). *The emerging network: A sociology of the new age and neo-pagan movements.* Lanham, MD: Rowman and Littlefield.

*Young practitioners' tales: Daily cultivation practice of kids at Minghui Dou Dou Kindergarten in Taiwan (Photos).* (2005). Retrieved May 1, 2008, from http:// www.pureinsight.org/pi/index.php?news=3211

Zablocki, B., & Looney, J. A. (2004). Research on new religious movements in the post-9/11 world. In P. C. Lucas & T. Robbins (Eds.), *New religious movements in the twenty-first century* (pp. 313-328). New York: Routledge.

Zeng, J. (2006). *Witnessing history: One Chinese woman's fight for freedom.* New York: Soho.

Zheng, Z. (2006). *A scientific discovery: "Five sounds make a man deaf."* Retrieved April 20, 2008, from http://www.pureinsight.org/pi/index. php?news=3753

Zhi, Y. (2006). *Canada: Members of Parliament support Falun Gong in condemning the CCP's live organ harvesting (Photos).* Retrieved April 20, 2008, from http:// www.clearwisdom.net/emh/articles/2006/9/28/78449.html

Zohar. (2003). *The Zohar* (Revised Edition ed. Vol. 1-23). Los Angeles: The Kabbalah Centre International, Inc.

三十六計. (2008). 三十六計: 走為上策. Retrieved April 30, 2008, from http:// www. minghui-school.org/school/article/category8,0.html

不惑. (2003a). 明慧學校教案(17)— 詩歌：日內瓦湖邊的清晨. Retrieved April 30, 2008, from http://www.minghui-school.org/school/article/2003/10/17/ 25456. html

不惑. (2003b). 明慧學校教案(18)— 畫畫：日內瓦湖邊的清晨. Retrieved April 30, 2003, from http://www.minghui-school.org/school/article/2003/10/ 20/25512.html

九集電視. (2008). 九集電視記錄片: 我們告訴未來(七)--艱難歲月. Retrieved April 30, 2008, from http://www.minghui-school.org/school/article/subcategory 710. html

女媧. (2004). 明慧學校教案(26)：女媧造人煉石補天. Retrieved April 30, 2008, from http://www.minghui-school.org/school/article/2003/10/17/25456.html

孔融讓梨. (2003). 明慧學校教案(19)— 孔融讓梨. Retrieved April 30, 2008, from http://www.minghui-school.org/school/article/2003/12/8/27135.html

我声明. (n.d.). 我声明退出共产党和共产党其它组织. Retrieved December 29, 2008, from http://tuidang.epochtimes.com

明慧學校交流園地. (2008). 明慧學校交流園地. Retrieved April 30, 2008, from http://school.mh4u.org/index.php?site=school

梁淑萍. (2005). 明慧學校教案(46): 明代. Retrieved April 30, 2008, from http:// www.minghui-school.org/school/article/2005/6/18/44963.html

歌曲. (2008). 歌曲:星星的故事. Retrieved April 30, 2008, from http://www. ming-hui-school.org/school/article/subcategory910.html

鍾俊妃. (2003). 明慧學校教案(12) - 中秋節. Retrieved April 30, 2008, from http:// www.minghui-school.org/school/article/2003/9/13/24522.html

高雄明慧學校. (2005). 明慧學校教案(35)：植物的超感功能. Retrieved April 30, 2008, from http://www.minghui-school.org/school/article/2005/2/2/ 40741.html

# Index


alienation, 21, 29, 109
assess, 90, 130
assessment, 91

banknotes, 74. *See also* money
book, 33, 43, 48-50, 52, 66-68, 74, 88, 105
brain, the, 25-27
brainstorm, xi, 103
brainwash, 8, 28, 77
Buddha Fa, 8. *See also* Buddha Law
Buddha Law, 5, 8, 10. *See also* Buddha
    Fa; Falun Dafa; Falun Gong

CCRM, 112-13, 115-19, 121. *See also*
    revitalization movement
character, 3, 8-9, 10, 42, 54, 56, 66,
    90-91, 96-97, 113-14. *See also* mind-
    nature; temperament
chatting, 78-79. *See also* texting
Chinese School, 99-100, 105-7
circumventing censorship, 67, 79-80
circumventing firewalls, 51-52, 71
cold calling, 50, 76, 78
compassion,  34, 42-43, 50, 53-56, 59-
    61, 63-67, 69-70, 74, 86, 93-94, 96,
    113, 118-20, 129
conversion, 2, 9, 14, 41-42, 44-46, 48,
    50-51, 54, 60, 63, 68, 70, 80, 87,
    113-15, 117, 120

crackdown, 6, 12, 25, 77
cross-cultural revitalization movement
    *See* CCRM
cross-cultural, 34, 106-7, 110-12, 116-17
cult, 3, 8-9, 16, 21, 25

Dafa, 5, 65-66, 83, 88, 97
data analysis, 32, 34, 38
data collection, 32, 33, 35, 39, 80
declarations, 81-84
delimitations, 38, 45
demonstrate, 47
demonstrations, 45, 47, 56, 60, 71, 85-
    86, 112
demonstrators, 6
deprivation, 19-22, 24-26, 28-29, 109,
    116. *See also* relative deprivation
Deprive, 20, 26
description, 8, 13-14, 20, 73, 100
digital guerilla, 42, 60, 80, 86
digital invasion, 81
Divine Performing Arts, 9, 11, 72. *See*
    *also* Shenyun
drama, 47, 63, 85, 90-91, 95, 97
draw, 88
drawing, 56, 93-95, 97

e-mail, 33-34, 51, 53, 63, 77, 79, 81
educate, 2, 25, 34, 117

education, 2, 8, 13, 33-35, 37-39, 48,
    54, 56, 60, 79-80, 89-90, 95-96, 100,
    102, 110, 116-20, 123-24, 126-27
educational, 1-2, 7-8, 33, 39, 52, 70, 95-
    97, 99, 102, 104, 117-18, 120
endurance, 11, 60. *See also* tolerance,
    forbearance
ethical, 20, 35
evaluation, 120. *See also* self-evaluation

Fa, 11-12, 71, 96, 113-14
Falun Dafa, 5-6, 8-10, 64, 66, 69-70, 74,
    76-77. *See also* Buddha Law
Falun, 5, 9, 10, 49, 71, 97
five exercises, 10, 42, 44, 56, 59, 63, 67
forbearance, 11, 64. *See also* tolerance,
    endurance
funding, 55, 78

geopolitics, 111
global movements, 13, 22
global, 19, 23-24, 28, 52-53, 60, 80, 86,
    106, 112, 119
globalization, 22-23, 28
globalized, 19, 28, 39
gong, 66, 91
Grounded Theory, xi, 2, 13, 31-32, 35,
    38-39, 41, 115
growth, 7, 13, 41-42, 44, 46, 50-51, 55,
    59-60, 63, 68, 74, 78, 80, 87, 100-
    102, 104, 106, 110, 113-14, 120

history, 3-4, 17, 22, 39, 49, 59, 74, 83,
    88-89, 91, 93, 97, 106, 112, 118

immorality, 80
imperative, 104, 119-20
informed consent, 35, 123, 125
interconnected, 53, 111
interconnectedness, 22, 53
Internet, 7, 24, 33, 37, 42, 50-53, 66-68,
    74-75, 78-80, 82, 87, 94-95, 117-18
interview, xi, 7, 11, 28, 33-39, 41-45,
    47, 49-61, 63, 65, 68, 71, 73-74, 101,
    112, 128-31

Kabbalah, 102, 104-7, 115-16
karma, 10, 12, 64-66, 71, 80
Korean School, 101, 105-7

law body, 9-10, 66, 70, 96. *See also*
    wheel
lawsuits, 84-86
legend, 56, 58-59, 91, 95, 97
lesson plan, 88-90
level, 3, 5, 9-10, 12-13, 15, 17, 25, 33,
    37, 41-43, 46, 55, 58, 65, 66, 79, 90,
    101-3, 105, 111, 114, 127, 129
Li Hongzhi, 5, 7, 23, 87, 120
limitations, 2, 24, 39
Los Angeles, 38, 53, 72, 75, 87, 99-102,
    105-6
lotus, 12

marketing, 79, 86
Master Li, 8-12, 52, 63-71, 83, 88, 94-
    96, 118. *See also* Li Hongzhi
media, 4-5, 7-8, 11-12, 33, 36, 38, 42,
    48, 51-53, 60-61, 63, 65-69, 71, 73-
    79, 84, 86, 94
meditating, 10, 26, 88
meditation, 3-4, 12, 26, 42, 44, 60, 65,
    68, 86, 94-95, 97, 104, 117-20
meditative, 44
memorization, 96-97, 101, 117-19
metacognition, 96-97, 118-20
metacognitive, 65, 117
method, CCRMs, 116
method, Chinese school, 100
method, FLG, 7, 20, 45, 47, 53, 58, 60-
    61, 66, 69, 74, 86-88, 94-97, 112-13,
    115, 117-18
method, Kabbalah, 102-3
method, Korean school, 101
method, qigong, 4
method, research, xi, 2, 35, 38, 115
method, transferable, 120
methodology, research, 19, 26, 29, 31,
    32-39
Ming Hui complementary curriculum,
    56, 88

Ming Hui content, 59, 91
Ming Hui methodology, 94
Ming Hui network, 87
Ming Hui school site, 88, 93
Ming Hui School, 36, 49, 52-60, 68, 86-97, 99-107, 113-14, 117-19, 130-31
Ming Hui, 11
model, 18, 31, 34, 38, 54, 56, 67, 111, 113-15
modernization, 21, 24, 29, 109-10, 116
money, 22-23, 46, 48-49, 52, 70, 74, 77, 86, 92, 113. *See also* banknotes
moral, 11, 21, 34, 42, 58, 66, 81, 90, 92-93, 100, 110-14, 116-17, 119
morality, 47, 95, 112
multiple intelligences, 95, 97, 117, 119
myth, 56, 59, 72, 91, 95, 97

Nativistic Movements, 13-15, 21, 109
network, 19, 23, 28, 42, 46, 60, 63, 67, 84, 86, 94, 99, 112, 117-19. *See also* Ming Hui Network
networking, 20, 80, 84-85, 115
New Religious Movements. *See* NRM
new vision, 95, 97, 111, 113, 115, 117
newspaper, 33, 48-49, 52, 63-64, 66, 75, 77-78
nine day seminars, 69
NRM, 8, 12-14, 18-19, 21, 24-25, 31

observations, 28, 33, 35, 37-38

pain, 11-12, 97
parades, 47, 71-72, 86
parents, xi, 34, 36, 53-56, 59-60, 89, 101, 119, 131
park, 1, 35, 37, 42, 44, 47, 60, 68-69, 86, 88, 117
participants, xi, 9, 32-37, 39, 44-45, 47-49, 51-52, 63, 123-24
poetic, 59
poetry, 58, 93-94, 97
political, 2, 7-8, 16, 19, 22, 29, 33, 47, 58, 65, 72, 83-86, 93, 115, 117
politically, 14

politics, 23-24, 49, 67
practitioners, 1, 4-7, 9-14, 18, 21, 24-26, 34, 36-39, 41-56, 59, 64-78, 84-85, 87-89, 92, 94-95, 105, 111, 113, 117-19, 128-29
principal, 36, 49, 54-59, 130
print, 42, 48, 50, 63, 74-75
printing, 24
problem statement, 2

qi gong. *See* qigong
qi, 1, 4
qigong, 1-6, 9-12, 34, 69, 109
qualitative, research, 2, 31-32, 39
questionable, 95
questionnaire, 35, 127
questions, 7, 13-15, 17, 19, 24-25, 32, 34-35, 36, 49, 51-52, 54, 69-70, 87-88, 91, 94, 97, 99, 101, 103-4, 111, 123-24. *See also* research questions

Rational Choice, 19, 22, 25, 29, 109
reception, 97
rectify, 65
rectifying the Fa, 11, 65
rectifying, 11
Relative Deprivation, 19-20, 24-25, 109
religion, 1, 3-4, 7-9, 11, 13-14, 16, 19-23, 25-27, 41, 83-85, 89, 106, 110-12, 115
reports before governments, 85
research questions, 2, 38, 109, 117
restoration, 60, 63
restore, 4, 58, 112
results, 39, 41, 43-61, 63-86
revitalization movement, 2, 8, 13, 15-18, 106, 109-12, 115
Revitalization theory, 13-15, 17-18, 28, 109, 121
revitalize, 105, 110, 112

sample, 32, 37, 63, 89
science, 6-7, 12, 14, 25, 27, 94-95, 97, 110
secular media, 52, 73

secularization, 19, 21, 24-25, 28-29,
    109, 116
secularized, 23, 25, 119
self-assessment, 91, 96-97
self-evaluation, 95, 119
semi-structured interviews, 36
setting, 37, 68
share, 6, 34, 42, 50-51, 71, 77, 89, 103,
    113, 117, 119
sharing, xi, 42, 45-48, 50-51, 56, 60, 63,
    65-66, 68, 70-71, 74, 86, 101-2, 112,
    117-18, 119
shenyun, 9, 11, 56-57. *See also* Divine
    Performing Arts
shows, 47-48, 73, 100-101
significance, 7
significant, 14, 22, 39, 48, 52, 56, 112,
    115
socialization, 8, 32, 37, 39, 41-61, 63-
    87, 112-15, 118
socio-political, 13, 21, 107
Southern California, 7, 11, 18, 39, 45,
    47, 75, 99, 111, 114
spiritual, 2, 8, 18, 22, 24, 27, 34, 42,
    44-45, 49, 80, 83-84, 96-97, 104-7,
    115, 121
spirituality, 24, 34, 96, 102-3
stories, 1, 8, 34, 42, 45-46, 56, 63, 71,
    73-74, 88-89, 91, 93, 95, 97, 103, 117
suffer, 5, 8, 10-12, 21, 60, 66, 84, 93

telephone, 33, 42, 50, 63, 76-79
telephones, 33, 42, 50, 63, 76-79
temperament, 8, 54, 59. *See also*
    character, mind-nature

text, 12-13, 33, 36, 38, 48-50, 53, 58-60,
    67, 73, 74, 78-79, 81-83, 86, 89-90,
    96, 100, 102, 105-6, 118-19
textbook, 49, 100
texting, 78-79, 81 86
tolerance, 42-43, 50, 53, 55-56, 59-61,
    63-64, 66-67, 69-70, 86, 90, 93,
    96-97, 113, 118-20, 129. *See also*
    endurance, forbearance
transmission, 96-97, 106, 117-18
truth-clarification, 65
truth-news, 67
truth-telling, 42, 44, 65-66
truth, 12, 34, 42, 46-49, 54, 59, 63-66,
    70, 73-74, 76, 81, 93, 102-105, 112,
    115, 118, 120, 129
truthfulness, 8-9, 11-12, 43, 50, 53, 55-
    56, 59-61, 63-64, 67, 69, 86, 93, 96-
    97, 113, 119

validating the Fa, 11-12, 33, 113-14
virtue, 10, 12, 59, 66, 71
vision, 42, 52, 59, 106, 110, 112, 117
visions, 22, 26, 97, 129
volunteer, 45, 54, 70, 75, 82, 87, 105,
    113, 115, 119
volunteerism, 42, 45, 60, 63, 69-71, 86,
    112, 114-16, 119

wheel, 5, 9-10, 64, 96. *See also* law
    body
White Lotus, 3, 39, 106

Zhuan Falun, 5, 8-10, 12-13, 42, 46, 48-
    52, 59, 64, 66-67, 74, 88